CHARLES DICKENS
The Writer and his Work

a *Writers and their Work* Special
in the critical and bibliographical series
General Editor Ian Scott-Kilvert

By Permission of The Tate Gallery   D. Maclise

CHARLES DICKENS

The Writer and his Work

by

BARBARA HARDY

PUBLISHED BY
PROFILE BOOKS LTD
WINDSOR, BERKSHIRE, ENGLAND

First Published 1983
Profile Books Ltd
Windsor, Berks
© *Barbara Hardy 1983*

Printed by
Unwin Brothers Limited,
The Gresham Press, Old Woking, Surrey
England

ISBN 0 85383 598 5

CONTENTS

CHARLES DICKENS

INTRODUCTION

One of the greatest modern writers, James Joyce, claimed
that Dickens has entered into the language more than any
writer since Shakespeare.[1] This is not mere praise. Like
Shakespeare, Dickens brims with originality, but expresses and addresses human nature at large. Like
Shakespeare, he is fully in possession of himself, creating
an art that is powerfully personal and generously
accessible. Like Shakespeare, he creates a flexible
language for self-expression and imaginative creativity
that commands admiration for its brilliance and virtuosity.
Like Shakespeare, he creates a unique and independent-
seeming world, allowing us to use that time-worn term
'world' with precision.

Dickens has entered into the art and consciousness of
modern writers such as Joyce, T. S. Eliot, Evelyn Waugh,
George Orwell, and Angus Wilson, but has also been
assimilated without too much damage into popular
culture and media such as film, radio, and television. His
myths are old and new, Victorian and modern. Pickwick,
Mrs. Gamp, Quilp, and Oliver Twist are only a few of his
many popular fictions, individual and typical, comic and
terrible. Such characters can stand as models or reminders
of his own genius, for, like their author, they combined
peculiarity with ordinariness. Their ancestors are Falstaff,
Lady Macbeth, Iago, and Hamlet; like them, they speak
with the force and simplicity of moral abstractions but are
imagined as individuals with appropriate voice and form.
They carry history with them: it is hard to think of the
wretched Victorian orphan or the workhouse without

[1]'The Centenary of Charles Dickens,' in *Journal of Modern
Literature*, 5, no. 1 (February 1976).

remembering Oliver and his porridge bowl, of the Victorian capitalist without remembering Dombey and his son, of sly or brutal crime without remembering Fagin and Bill Sikes, of prison without remembering the Dorrits, of the newly rich without remembering the Veneerings, of cant and prudishness without Podsnap. Their very names are vivid metonymies. For many readers, Dickens is not only a great novelist but a history book. Victorian England is his 'best of times' and 'worst of times,' though the sentence in which he used those words at the beginning of *A Tale of Two Cities* (1859) was not referring to his epoch or his society. His fictions are packed with social information and social passion.

LIFE

Although he is a great entertainer and comic genius, we have come to know him as a famous example of the wounded artist, whose sicknesses were shed in great art, whose very grudges against family and society linked him through personal pains with larger public sufferings. Dickens was born in Landport, Portsea, on 7 February 1812, second son of John Dickens, a clerk in the Navy Pay Office, whose improvidence led to imprisonment in the Marshalsea for debt. Dickens was sent to work at the age of twelve in Warren's Blacking Warehouse. After his

Hungerford Stairs Westminster, 1823; the building on the right is Warren's Blacking Warehouse   G. Harley & G. Dighton

father's release he went back to school, then into an attorney's office. He spent much of his time exploring the busy and varied life of London and decided to become a journalist. He mastered a difficult system of shorthand and by March 1832, at the age of twenty, he was a general and parliamentary reporter. His father's fecklessness became the comic insouciance of Micawber; the prison became a fictional fact and a myth; the humiliation was a creative obsession; the journalism was his apprenticeship. In 1829 he met and soon fell in love with Maria Beadnell, but her parents found him socially inferior: her looks and temperament, their young love, and his subsequent encounter with her in middle age provided the bitter-sweet tones and trials of David Copperfield's love for Dora and the not-quite-blighted exuberance of Flora Finching in *Little Dorrit* (1855–1857). After Dickens joined the *Morning Chronicle* in 1833, his first sketch, 'A Dinner at Poplar,' was published, and others followed. He travelled the country reporting meetings and by-elections, enjoyed a rapidly expanding social life, and in April 1836, two months after the publication of *Sketches by Boz*, married Catherine Hogarth. He next contracted to write a serial, which became *Pickwick Papers* (1836–1837), and, with the death of the artist Seymour, began his long association with Phiz. He had already agreed to edit *Bentley's Miscellany*, in which *Oliver Twist* appeared in 1837–1839.

Early in 1837 the first of his ten children was born, and in May Catherine's sister Mary, who had lived with them since their marriage, died. Dickens' intense grief was memorialized in the nearly fatal illness of Rose Maylie in *Oliver Twist*, and lasted until his death. In 1838 he visited the 'cheap schools of Yorkshire,' about which he wrote in *Nicholas Nickleby* (1838–1839), and about this time he met the philanthropist Angela Burdett Coutts and put his social concern and energy to work for her causes. They established a Home for Fallen Women in 1847. By the late 1830's he was a literary lion, but his radical intensity survived success and social prestige, and he continued to

Dickens delivers his first newspaper article

Catherine Dickens   D. Maclise

attack privilege, patronage, snobbery, injustice and inhumanity.

Having expanded the original idea of *Master Humphrey's Clock* (1840–1841) – papers supposedly written in a weekly gathering and put in an old-fashioned clock kept in Master Humphrey's queer old house – into the full-length narrative of *The Old Curiosity Shop* (1840–1841) and at last got down to the writing of *Barnaby Rudge* (1841), Dickens continued to voice his detestation of the employment of children in the mines and condemned factory conditions, writing lampoons against the Tories who opposed humane legislation. In 1842 he visited America. Fêted and lionized to the point of exhaustion, he found much to praise and much to hate, and *American Notes* (1842) and *Martin Chuzzlewit* (1843–1844) were fed by his violently mixed responses. In 1844–1845 he went to Italy, where the bells of Genoa provided him with the title for *The Chimes* (1844), the 'little book' that struck ' a great blow for the poor.' On his return he had a short period as editor of the *Daily News* and campaigned for improvements in the Ragged Schools (voluntary institutions providing free instruction for children of the poor) and for the abolition of public hangings.

Dombey and Son (1846–1848) was written partly in Paris and Lausanne, and after *David Copperfield* (1848–1850) Dickens started his own magazine, *Household Words*, whose tone and temper were his own – humanitarian and radical. Authorial and editorial activities were somehow combined with amateur theatricals, frequently in aid of charity. In 1851 he moved to Tavistock House, which was large enough for his family (and for the Hogarths, his wife's family, when he was away), and began *Bleak House* (1852–1853) in the following year. At Christmas 1853 he read *A Christmas Carol* (1843) to an audience of 2,000; and the next year the falling sales of *Household Words* were boosted by the publication of *Hard Times* (1854). Dickens pleaded urgently in his magazine for improvements in sanitation

13

following the cholera epidemic in 1854.

He pilloried Palmerston and the government for the appalling mis-management of the Crimean War, the central attack on inefficiency being sustained in *Little Dorrit* (1855-1857). He bought the house that he had coveted since childhood, Gad's Hill Place, near Rochester, but by 1857 it was becoming clear that his marriage was at an end. He turned frantically to the idea of undertaking a series of readings from his books, but the crisis with Catherine had been reached. Urged by her mother, she left him, and rumours got abroad that Ellen Ternan, a young actress whom he had met during his production of Wilkie Collins' *The Frozen Deep*, was his mistress. This provoked Dickens to a public and personal assertion of their innocence, a famous and characteristic act of indiscretion.

In April 1859 he brought out a new magazine, *All the Year Round*, which opened with *A Tale of Two Cities*, but sales fell, and it needed *Great Expectations* (1860-1861) to restore them. Dickens' creative restlessness continued, but with more and more manic public readings his health deteriorated. After the mid-1860's Ellen Ternan stayed periodically at Gad's Hill. On 9 June 1865 Dickens was involved in a railway accident that is mentioned in the postscript to *Our Mutual Friend* (1864-1865), but he went on reading, even going to America in 1867-1868. Financially successful but physically battered, he refused to heed the warnings – partial paralysis, inability to read street signs on his left side, increasing lameness in the left foot – and undertook another series of readings in 1870. On 15 March he gave a last reading of *A Christmas Carol*. He died on 9 June 1870, leaving *Edwin Drood* unfinished, in a final *coup de théatre*.

Like all lives, Dickens' is full of loose ends and contradictions. He is the great novelist of childhood, whose demands and disappointments alienated his own children; the great sentimental celebrant of domestic life, whose separation from his wife incurred painful publicity; the defender of sexual morals, whose love for Ellen

Ellen Ternan with her husband 1883

Ternan stimulated speculations of every kind. He was also a novelist who loved to devise plots that hinged on secrecy and disclosure and who succeeded in keeping secret his own private life. As an amateur of detection, he might have enjoyed or deplored the literary detective work that has failed to discover the nature of his relationship with Ellen Ternan. K. J. Fielding suggested (in his British Council pamphlet on Dickens, *Writers and Their Work* series, no. 37) that Dickens' critics have not used recent biographical revelations with precision and definiteness; and this is still true, with the exception of Angus Wilson and Michael Slater. Dickens' later heroines, for instance, are too often crudely identified as images of Ellen, and though her name connects itself irresistibly with the names of Estella, Bella, and Helena Landless, their originality and spirit were not new in his novels. Edith Dombey and Louisa Gradgrind are also brilliantly lucid instances of their author's insight into women's sexuality, aggression, and pride, and of his capacity to bring out these qualities in ideological, as well as psychological, significance. Dickens' life was not at all like a Dickens novel, though his energy, his egocentricity, and his histrionic virtuosity mark both the life and the work.

SKETCHES BY BOZ

Dickens' career has twin stamps of power. The end is plainly present in the beginning, and the end has progressed far beyond the beginning. Great artists find forms for their individuality, while always exhibiting that improvability so rare in human experience. Like many other novelists – Defoe, Richardson, Fielding, Thackeray, George Eliot, Zola, and Henry James – Dickens began as a journalist, then moved from fact to fiction. Like his own David Copperfield, he first wrote in bondage to other men's words. His work as a parliamentary reporter trained him in attention, speed, and precision. As he listened and wrote, he was educating his response to words, rhythms, eloquence, and personality. From reporting, he moved on to the freer forms of journalism, and *Sketches by Boz* provides us with a collection of essays that shows the evolution of the prose writer, the storyteller, the creator of character, and the analyst of environments and objects. Of course, Dickens never gave up journalism, and his career as a novelist developed together with editorial labours, journalistic essays, and speeches. But *Sketches by Boz* offers a lucid example of a novelist learning and developing his special novelistic powers. We could turn this statement on its head and praise *Sketches* as great journalism, sharp in observation, animated in language, recording signs while interpreting their meanings. However, there is more to this book than impressive reporting.

Dickens is a dynamic presenter of the world of the city. At times it seems as if the actual environment of rapid social and economic change helped to develop his mastery of flux. In *Sketches* we see an energetic meeting of artist and subject. Whatever building, street, or institution Dickens describes, he more than describes. He is a vivid observer of the mobility of surfaces, and the many surfaces in *Sketches by Boz* are truthfully designed not to be static. Dickens knows that so-called solid objects do not present themselves in a still world, but as moving aspects of social mutability. He seizes and particularizes moments and movements. When he describes dirty London streets, for instance, in chapter 2 of the section entitled 'The Streets – Night,' we are told that 'just enough damp' is 'gently stealing down' to make the pavements greasy. The gas lamps are said to look more luminous because of 'the heavy lazy mist, which hangs over every object.' Description in *Sketches* is consistently cinematic, animated by Dickens' refusal to paint a static scene. Where there is an apparent exception, it proves the rule, since its stillness is emphatic. Here is a short description of a room that is waiting for a tenant, and thus is unnaturally void and placid:

Street Scene: London's Poor   Gustave Doré

It was a neat, dull little house, on the shady side of the way, with new, narrow floorcloth in the passage, and new, narrow stair-carpets up to the first floor. The paper was new, and the paint was new, and the furniture was new; and all three, paper, paint, and furniture, bespoke the limited means of the tenant. There was a little red and black carpet in the drawing room, with a border and flooring all the way round; a few stained chairs and a Pembroke table. A pink shell was displayed on each of the little sideboards, which, with the addition of a tea-tray and caddy, a few more shells on the mantelpiece, and three peacock's feathers tastefully arranged above them, completed the decorative furniture of the apartment.[2]

('Our Parish,' ch. 7)

Dickens, like Henry James, knew that human beings can't be separated from their personal environments of clothes, accessories, furniture, rooms, and houses. The only cold, still things are those waiting to be peopled. There is a sense in which even this quiet scene refuses to stay quite still. Its quietness is a Dickensian quietness, alert and tense. This is an early essay, but its language is strikingly Dickensian, in insistent repetition and mounting rhythm, which transforms fact into poetry. Dickens has an eye for the odd particular, like the pink shell and the peacock feathers, which not only provide selective vividness and focus but convey a precise sense of social ways and means. The eye and voice of the mature Dickens are apparent from his very first exercises, despite occasional uneconomical phrasing. Here is the germ of the bravura set pieces of the late Dickens, the repetitions that stylise and signify the veneer of the Veneerings in *Our Mutual Friend*, though he is as yet relatively restrained, unpractised in exaggeration and in the stylizations that mark the poetic prose of the later novels.

Although Dickens is not yet engaged with psychological subtlety, the 'I' of his anonymous but animated reporter has some psychological dimension. The observer here is constantly recording and responding to social change.

[2]All quotations from the works are from *The New Oxford Illustrated Dickens*, 21 vols. (London, 1947–1958).

Scotland Yard, for instance, like most of the places and buildings, is described historically, in terms of what it was and what it has become during a specified period of time. The observer in *Sketches* is closely attentive to the erosions and accretions that unbuild and rebuild a great city, changing the scene from day to day, if we watch with conscientious concentration. This sense of historical motion is one of the remarkable achievements of *Sketches* and is recognizably a beginning of a form and a theme that continue throughout the novels, rising into prominence in *Dombey and Son* and later works. But it is given individuality and personality by being attached to personal memory. History is vivid here because it is observed through particular eyes, particular ears, and a particular memory.

It is also presented through an intelligent inference of the future from the past, active and impassioned. Dickens makes his novelist-character David Copperfield observe that observation may be called a quality of creative power. David is provided with marvellously vivid things to observe and makes us observe them as signifiers of Dickens' power: the tall fowls, the greenness of the churchyard's grass, the wrinkled wax Peggotty kept for her thread, the workbox with a view of St. Paul's pink dome, and the rough red of Peggotty's skin blended with the smooth red velvet of the parlour footstool. All these things are described as objects originally observed, well enough in the past to be remembered. The novelist makes his novelist fully comprehend this process: 'If it should appear from anything I may set down in this narrative that I was a child of close observation, or that as a man I have a strong memory of my childhood, I undoubtedly lay claim to both of these characteristics.'

The descriptions in *Sketches* are individualized by Dickens' brilliant layering of visual experience: objects and places are not visualized baldly, as if seen for the first time, or for a once-and-only time. They are objects seen as remembered. This complication of simple visual record is not only animated but true to writing experience, which superimposes image on experience. Objects in fiction are inevitably remembered, and rely, too, on the reader's memory. Dickens' wandering Londoner also introduces a further layer of comparative experience. The author analyzes the activity of intelligence and imagination:

We never see any very large, staring, black Roman capitals, in a book, or shop-window, or placarded on a wall, without their immediately recalling to our mind an indistinct and confused recollection of the time when we were first initiated in the mysteries of the alphabet. We almost fancy we see the pen's point following the letter, to impress its form more strongly on our bewildered imagination; and wince involuntarily, as we remember the hard knuckles with which the reverend old lady who instilled into our mind the first principles of education for ninepence per week, or ten and sixpence per quarter, was wont to poke our juvenile head occasionally, by way of adjusting the confusion of ideas in which we were generally involved. The same kind of feeling pursues us in many other instances, but there is no place which recalls so strongly our recollections of childhood as Astley's. It was not a 'Royal Amphitheatre' in those days, nor had Ducrow arisen to shed the light of classic taste and portable gas over the sawdust of the circus; but the whole character of the place was the same, the pieces were the same, the clown's jokes were the same, the riding-masters were equally grand, the comic performers equally witty, the tragedians equally hoarse, and the 'highly-trained chargers' equally spirited. Astley's has altered for the better – we have changed for the worse. Our histrionic taste is gone, and with shame we confess, that we are far more delighted and amused with the audience, than with the pageantry we once so highly appreciated.

('Scenes,' ch. 11)

This apparently straightforward introduction is far from simple: it joins the two experiences of childhood learning and childhood play, through a deceptively informal and rambling structure of recall, which masks analysis and abstraction in a characteristically Dickensian fashion. If we compare Dickens with George Eliot or Marcel Proust, he is relaxed, informal, unanalytic, but the effect of the particulars he relates is essentially identical with the explicit concepts they articulate and generalize. It is easy to underrate Dickens' intelligence, because his habit is hardly ever that of analytic or generalized discourse. His vivid particulars are cunningly linked in contrasts and comparisons that reveal psychological intuition by the very way in which he inquires, answers, suggests, and informs. Not that conceptual language is absent: notice the careful use of phrases like 'indistinct and confused recollection,' 'we almost fancy,' and 'bewildered imagination.'

Sketches by Boz is also animated by Dickens' range of comedy. The theatrical influence, which many critics have noticed, is shown very clearly in the sketch of Astley's in chapter 11. Dickens describes comedy in a way that seems infected by the experience he reports. His actresses and clowns are larger than life, but the exaggeration and mannerism are surely inspired by their actual theatrical origins. A personal sense of the ridiculous is always available: the observer moves rapidly from precise theatrical report, amused and amusing, to travesty and fantasy: 'By the way, talking of fathers, we should very much like to see some piece in which all the *dramatis personae* were orphans. Fathers are invariably great nuisances on the stage'. 'By the way' introduces a casual-seeming digression, which expands and generates drama as Dickens rapidly throws off two tiny, funny, scornful scenes of implausible family discovery, complete with stagey dialogue and gesture:

'It is now nineteen years, my dear child, since your blessed mother (here the old villain's voice falters) confided you to my charge. You were then an infant,' &c., &c. Or else they have to discover, all of a sudden, that somebody whom they have been in constant communication with, during three long acts, without the slightest suspicion, is their own child: in which case they exclaim, 'Ah! what do I see? This bracelet! That smile! These documents! Those eyes! Can I believe my senses? – It must be! – Yes – it is, it is my child!' – 'My father!' exclaims the child; and they fall into each other's arms, and look over each other's shoulders, and the audience give three rounds of applause.

('Scenes,' ch. 11)

Dickens' affective range includes pathos as well as fun. One of the most interesting seminal sketches, 'The Pawnbroker's Shop,' shows this pathos at its best, not existing as a crude rhetorical device to force strong response from the reader, but dramatized in a compressed vignette that arrives at sympathy through analysis. There is analysis as well as persuasion, forcing understanding as well as pity. At the end of this sketch Dickens uses a scenic division and contrast (a device he develops in the novels). In a split-scene sketch of the shop he describes two girls, one still virtuous and the other 'whose attire, miserably poor but extremely gaudy...bespeaks her station.' The virtuous girl, with her mother, is pawning a gold chain and a 'forget-me-not' ring, and the prostitute catches sight of the trinkets and bursts into tears, in a variation of the theme of Holman Hunt's *The Awakening Conscience* (1851–1853). Dickens is carefully using a sentimental genre-piece in order to make a point about social corruption. The narrator infers that the first girl is no novice, because of the way she and her mother answer questions and bargain with the pawnbroker. They have some delicacy, standing back to 'avoid the observation even of the shopman' but are not too humiliated, 'for want has hardened the mother, and her example has hardened the girl, and the prospect of receiving money, coupled with a recollection of the misery they have both endured from the want of it,' has made them what they are. The prostitute represents a further stage in what Dickens calls degradation, but we are told that there are still 'chords in the human heart' that vibrate to past associations. In case we have still not got the point or may mistake this for a stark contrast between virtue and vice, Dickens dissolves the antithesis and presents a series:

There has been another spectator, in the person of a woman in the common shop; the lowest of the low; dirty, unbonneted,

23

The Pawnbroker's Shop   Sketches by Boz
                                          G. Cruikshank

flaunting, and slovenly. Her curiosity was at first attracted by the little she could see of the group; then her attention. The half-intoxicated leer changed to an expression of something like interest, and a feeling similar to that we have described, appeared for a moment, and only a moment, to extend itself even to her bosom.

('Scenes,' ch. 23)

Being Dickens, he ends by explicit comment, asking 'how soon these women may change places' and seeing all three as representing different stages of deterioration. The act of reporting social conditions makes a discovery about social conditioning.

Sketches by Boz is a three-part collection, which grows in complexity and creativity, beginning with 'Our Parish,' moving into 'Scenes,' where description and animated topography are joined, and continuing with 'Characters.' The art of the novelist is developing. Some of the pieces in 'Characters' tilt the character sketch in the direction of narrative, as in 'The Misplaced Attachment of Mr. John Dounce,' and it seems inevitable that *Sketches* should conclude with the fiction of 'Tales.'

PICKWICK PAPERS

In some ways *Sketches* is, for all its discontinuity, morally and sociologically more unified and probing than *Pickwick Papers*. Begun as a series of sketches, *Pickwick Papers* came to achieve narrative unity and continuity, but in a form that often divides comedy from pathos. In the inset tales that are narrated or read, following the eighteenth-century tradition on which Dickens was reared, Pickwick and his friends are given a literary supplement to their tour of investigation. It is a dark, grim, tragic supplement, telling of madness, crime, death, poverty, and misery. Pickwick's responses are always tellingly obtuse. It is not until he is himself involved with the institutions of law and the prison that he begins to feel and understand. This may be a gradual discovery, made

25

by the author in the process of developing continuity, but the effect is to departmentalize the grim and the comic materials, as in Victorian melodrama. Still, the underworld is present, and Pickwick's innocence is not to remain intact. There are also other compressed but conspicuous assertions of the underworld, in the black humour of Jingle's telegraphese and Sam Weller's anecdotes, which present deaths, murders, marital disaster, servants' wretchedness, fear, pain, drugs, horror, in the guise of joke – 'There's nothin so refreshin as sleep, sir, as the servant-girl said afore she drank the egg-cupful of laudanum.'

For the most part, the comedy of the novel lies apart from its pathos, and the various kinds of comedy – jokes, farce, comedy of humours, visual anecdote, social satire – seem to lie apart from each other. The episodic structure of the action, with its many narrative interruptions, shows Dickens' form at its most informal, and Dickens himself declared that he thought of it 'as being a book by itself and quite unlike his other work.'[3] *Pickwick Papers* makes no use of fantasy in its main action but up to a point it can be, and frequently has been, read as a fable. But what kind of fable? It proffers pastoral and domestic symbols of the good life, and its events and characters present moral concepts through simplification. Social and psychological complication are avoided. Like fable, it has a simply extractable point, and the story of Pickwick's journey from innocence to experience makes no attempt to show the difficulties and subtleties of leading the good life or passing ethical judgments. Insofar as it is a fable, it permits an evasiveness that is not present in the later novels. Moreover, to call it a fable is to pick on certain features and ignore others, and much of the description and narration is weak and tedious. It is much easier to see the structure and statement of *Pickwick Papers* at a considerable distance from the full text itself,

[3]Phillip Collins, ed., *Dickens: Interviews and Recollections*, 2 vols. (London, 1981), vol. I, p. 163.

and if we are to understand and judge its individual qualities as a work of art, and if we are to see its place in Dickens' work, we should keep close to its detail and try to say something about its variety. We must not lay stress on its resemblance to *Don Quixote*,[4] or its mythical rendering of the Fall,[5] or its revelations of the transcendent possibilities of human goodness,[6] without acknowledging the existence of materials that do not fit into mythical patterns.

Much of the power of *Pickwick Papers* resides in parts rather than in the whole, and in parts not very strongly attached to each other in feeling or moral argument. Criticism and irony are present in its comedy, but by no means in all the comic scenes or in all the comic characters. Dickens is often conventional in his comedy of humours and in farce, though he is strong in comic and macabre wit, joke, and anecdote. Where the comedy is neither satiric nor dark, it is frequently arch, jolly, or sentimental, as in the cozily convivial Dingley Dell scenes, or the farcical episodes of Pickwick on the ice, or in the wrong double-bedded room, where the illustrator's vivid compression shows up the flatness and feebleness of the prose narrative, or the scenes displaying the humours of Tupman and Snodgrass, where neither character nor action has the satiric bite or comic power of the theatrical source in Ben Jonson.

Even if we grant Dickens the excuse of an awkwardly imposed and improvised form, in which he gradually discovered a theme and a continuity, *Pickwick Papers* is an erratic novel. The 'amusing and pleasant' adventures are sealed off, for most of the action, from the episodes showing want and misery. The grotesque and zany comedy of the Wellers, the Fat Boy, the medical students,

[4]Ernest Simmons, *Dostoevsky: The Making of a Novelist* (London, 1940), p. 210.
[5]W. H. Auden, *The Dyer's Hand and Other Essays* (London, 1963), 'Dingley Dell and The Fleet,' pp. 407–428.
[6]S. Marcus, *Dickens from Pickwick to Dombey* (London, 1965), 'The Blest Dawn,' pp. 13–53, particularly pp. 18 and 51–53.

Mr. Pickwick slides

Pickwick Papers
Phiz

Jingle and the lawyers allow Dickens' imagination of misery to appear, but in a fragmented and flippant form. The fragmentation has its significance, showing Dickens' divided vision of a society he deplored and individual possibilities he celebrated. Dingley Dell's final celebratory reconciliations, moreover, are triumphs of middle-class morality: Sam refuses to marry until it is convenient for his master, and Tony Weller tries to make over his money to Pickwick. The adventures of the Pickwick Club are neither Odyssean nor Quixotic. Dickens aspires toward social criticism, but seems to edit rather than assimilate the intransigent materials of social reality.

OLIVER TWIST

In writing *Oliver Twist* Dickens was influenced by 'Newgate' novels dealing with criminals, such as Bulwer Lytton's *Eugene Aram* (1832) and Ainsworth's *Rookwood* (1834), but despite Dickens' own tendency toward melodrama, *Oliver Twist* breaks new ground in moral purpose and realism.

In *Oliver Twist* the incorruptible innocence is that of youth, not age. Dickens takes up the subject of character conditioned by environment imaged in 'The Pawnbroker's Shop' and absent in *Pickwick*. Oliver is one of several angelic children – Nell, Barnaby, Paul, and Florence – who embody virtue. Their radiance and purity are heightened and threatened by the darkness and deformity that surround them. Dickens tells us that he wanted Oliver to represent the strength of virtue in the fallen world: he is neglected, imprisoned, and isolated. He wanders in an unknown country and an unknown city, picking up dangerous helpers and teachers. He is involved in cruelty, misery and nightmare, and his child's point of view, both realistically and symbolically innocent, brings us close to the sensations of helplessness and panic. It is easy to speak of Dickens' virtuous characters as emblematic – which they are – but it is essential to notice his affective powers, which are highly developed in *Oliver Twist*. Its control and unity of theme and feeling distinguish it sharply from *Sketches*, which for all its excellence was a collection of magazine and newspaper pieces,[7] blended by an original talent, and from *Pickwick Papers*, where power is generated slowly and remains fitful. I do not agree with those critics who locate the beginnings of a unified theme in *Martin Chuzzlewit*, which deals centrally with selfishness, or *Dombey and Son*, which deals with pride. It is true that Dickens spoke explicitly about giving these novels a ruling subject, and that in them he marshals scene, image, and character into illustrative action. But as D. H. Lawrence reminds readers who are inclined to trust overmuch in the artist, the proof lies in the tale, and *Oliver Twist* is as wholly bent on pursuing a subject as are the later novels, though more mutedly. That subject is the relationship of the individual to his environment, and it is one that Dickens considered, explicitly and implicitly, in all his subsequent novels. The focus on moral abstractions like selfishness and pride has overimpressed critics, from John Forster onward.

In the first chapter of *Oliver Twist* Dickens cunningly and movingly modulates from comedy to pathos and from pathos to satire. He takes us from the drunken old woman to the dying mother, exclaiming, 'Let me see the child, and die,' and the brusque, habituated, but not totally calloused doctor. Dickens is learning to break down the barriers between pathos and comedy, and in doing so achieves not only structural continuity but also a control of pathos. Such rapid switches help in all the later novels to hold together disparate effects, to provide variety and unity, and to give that double opportunity for comedy and pathos that Dickens admired in stage

---

[7]Beginning with 'A Dinner at Poplar Walk,' in *Monthly Magazine*, n.s. 16 (December 1833), pp. 617–624, and ending with 'Vauxhall Gardens by Day' (*Sketches by 'Boz'*), *Morning Chronicle*, n.s. no. 4 (26 October 1836).

melodrama. I don't want to make the act of combination sound mechanically adroit, because at its best it brings about imaginative cohesion. There are more powerful instances, as in the horrifying juxtapositions of Chadband's gross appetite and grosser language with the delicacy of Jo, his text, object, and victim, in *Bleak House*; or of the neighbourhood of Mrs. Sparsit to Louisa Bounderby's moral crisis in the storm, in *Hard Times*; or of the interwoven dark and light threads of feeling in Merdle's suicide, in *Little Dorrit*. But it is in *Oliver Twist* that we first feel that proximity of laughter and pity, or amusement and horror, so congenial to Dickens. There is more here than the thrilling emotional collocation or the earthing of satire and pathos. Dickens, like all great artists, analyzes as he creates, discovers as he entertains.

In the harsh humour of the opening workhouse scene of *Oliver Twist*, Dickens has left far behind the Fat Boy's simple rhetorical intent in *Pickwick Papers* to 'make our flesh creep.' His imagination puts together facets of a particular place at a particular time, a bad place at a bad time, an English workhouse just after the Poor Law Act of 1834. Through the brilliant sleights-of-hand of his metonymies, the edifice is built and peopled. There are the representatives of officialdom, moulded by their roles, face to face with the representatives of the poor, moulded by their conditions. Dickens' method is to make character illustrative while preserving it from abstraction. The characters in *Oliver Twist*, like the women in 'The Pawnbroker's Shop,' exhibit the hardening and perverting social process, a draining away of humanity. In the first chapter, mother and child are presented in the timeless anonymity of birth and death, through a single imperative, 'Let me see the child, and die.' The sentence is not banal speech. It sums up the mother's instinctive desire to see the newborn baby, and takes a short stride from birth to death: the two experiences encompassed in one sentence give this character a little life, but enough. The old pauper is presented with the same economy. She gives her grim advice, 'Think what it is to be a mother, there's a dear

31

young lamb, do' – exactly what Oliver's mother is doing – and reminisces in beery vein on her experiences of birth, death, and workhouse misery. And the doctor, drawing the official line at not 'being bothered' if the baby gives trouble, as he knows it's likely to do, is sufficiently deflected from his professional humour by a glint of particular response after he puts on 'his gloves with great deliberation': 'She was a good-looking girl, too; where did she come from?' The time and the place bring these people together; with apparently effortless art Dickens observes how time and place have made and unmade them.

Dickens' subject is conditioned human nature. At the centre of the moral action is the virtuous and innocent child, created in a successful blend of myth and particularity. The innocence of the child comes to the Victorian and modern reader out of Christian tradition and social fact, with the simple vividness of a famine poster. Its fabulous simplicity is supported by psychological vividness. One of Dickens' few strengths as a psychological novelist is his rendering of childhood sensibility. The idealized nature of Oliver is conveyed or licensed – neither metaphor is quite right – in a medium of feeling. Oliver feels timidity, starving bravado, isolation, horror, fear, relief, shame, nightmare, and loving reciprocity. These passions are animated in a continuum, to which the reader's response is fluent and varied. It is sometimes suggested – by Henry James, for instance – that Oliver's sustained gentlemanliness is unconvincing, and Dickens was himself uneasily aware that this might be so. But, as so often, he is straddling fable and realism. It was not his purpose to create a totally accurate portrait of a foundling, but to combine such a portrait with an image of original virtue.

Dickens shows Oliver's resistance and courage as the product of heredity, just as Shakespeare makes Perdita's royal nature transcend her rustic nurture, but there is more to Oliver's moral style than a romantic theory of heredity. Dickens' exploration of the conditioned character relies on the presence of a controlling fable or fantasy about the unconditioned and unconditional. From *Pickwick* onward there is a double vision: a vision of the power and terror of the real world and a vision of the power and glory of human love. The first vision is shown realistically, the second idealistically. After *Pickwick*, the ideal virtue is not presented so emblematically as to be set apart from the social environment in which it is placed. Oliver escapes the environment's dangers, as only angelic children may escape, but we feel the existence of a real threat. *Oliver Twist* is not only concerned with its hero, but with the perverted population that surrounds him. The members of the thieves' gang have different fates, marked on a descending scale. The brilliant child's play of Fagin's schooling is a paradigm of environment and conditioning. Rose Maylie and her protected middle-class world offer an escape to Nancy, much in the style of a paternalist employer or a welfare organization, but Nancy truthfully says that she was brought up in the streets and cannot get out of them. The tension between her environment and her struggling virtue kills her; the murder is no simple climax in a crime story or a moral tale, but tells a truth about a death struggle between nature and nurture, self and society.

The plot to corrupt Oliver is sometimes condemned for weakness and implausibility. It is true that explanation and exposition are huddled up at the end of the novel, but this novel is a social parable, and Monks's plot to corrupt his half brother is part of a total pattern that includes the workhouse, the baby farm, the thieves' den, the Brownlow home, and the criminality of Sikes. Dickens comes close to endangering Oliver's idealized virtue in the great temptation scene in chapter 18. The child is being carefully brainwashed, first cunningly cold-shouldered and isolated, then cunningly brought into the deadly warmth of the thieves' family circle. Here he shows all the susceptibility of the return from exile as clearly as, say, Rubashov, the hero of Arthur Koestler's *Darkness at Noon*. It is no good remembering the

Oliver's reception by Fagin and the boys

Oliver Twist
G. Cruikshank

diabolical suggestiveness of Fagin's fork if we forget the familiar sausage on its prong. Dickens symbolizes his moral action, but also domesticates it:

Oliver was but too glad to make himself useful; too happy to have some faces, however bad, to look upon; too desirous to conciliate those about him when he could honestly do so; to throw any objection in the way of this proposal. So he at once expressed his readiness; and, kneeling on the floor, while the Dodger sat upon the table so that he could take his foot in his lap, he applied himself to a process which Mr. Dawkins designated as 'japanning his trotter-cases.'

(ch. 18)

Oliver's invulnerability remains, but Dickens brings it into intimate connection with the brute force and insidious persuasiveness of a society that makes criminals. His is not an isolated fable. At the other extreme of the moral action is Sikes, who also shows Dickens' interest in corruptibility, as well as his insight as a derivation of complex human nature. Dickens describes Sikes as an utterly hardened character: 'Whether every gentler human feeling is dead within such bosoms, or the proper chord to strike has rusted and is hard to find, I do not pretend to know.'[8] And the extreme violence and resolution in outward action is fully expressive of the extremity of character.

If Dickens sees Sikes as dead or rusted in gentler human feelings, he most certainly does not show him only as the violently outraged and jealous murderer played on by events and by Fagin. The flight of Sikes is a behaviouristic display of strong but mixed and unclassified passions. The author contrives expressive actions that symbolize, precipitate, and blend the passions. The result is twofold: not only is tension sustained and renewed after the murder, but the interest is given a human focus, and the character of Sikes expands in a form of psychological melodrama where the stage is both interior and exterior. The events themselves are exciting: the pursuit, the

[8]From 'The Author's Preface to the Third Edition' (1841).

flight, the fire, the trap, the death. The inner register is also exciting and especially so for not being simple or predictable. Dickens is not showing us a brute nor indeed is he evoking easy compassion for a hunted man, but he is keeping Sikes (and us) in touch with certain common features of human feeling: loneliness, alienation, need for human contact and activity, repression, energy, and fear. Being Dickens, he uses a whole range of effects, from the ironic grim comedy of the cheapjack who finds the bloodstain on Sikes's hat to the symbolic fire-fighting at the end. In the fire we have the most successful external showing of something too subtle and complex to be analyzed or given a single name. Sikes seizes on the fire as an opportunity to use his energy and join it with that of other people. His is a pleasure, familiar in guilty or alienated states, in which participation in something detached from personal problems gives relief. Dickens also emphasizes the release of sheer physical brutality and loss of gentle human feeling. In Coleridgean terms we are kept on the 'highroad' of human passions and induced to feel a kind of sympathy, empathy rather than pity. The violent action is given an inner life of nerves and feelings.

For now, a vision came before him, as constant and more terrible than that from which he had escaped. Those widely staring eyes, so lustreless and so glassy, that he had better borne to see them than think upon them, appeared in the midst of the darkness; light in themselves, but giving light to nothing. There were but two, but they were everywhere. If he shut out the sight, there came the room with every well-known object – some, indeed, that he would have forgotten, if he had gone over its contents from memory – each in its accustomed place. The body was in *its* place, and its eyes were as he saw them when he stole away. He got up, and rushed into the field without. The figure was behind him. He re-entered the shed, and shrunk down once more. The eyes were there, before he had laid himself along.

(ch. 48)

So far this is brilliant criminal psychology: the involuntary imagery of strong passion realizes and substantiates the macabre presentation of the body with the carefully placed 'its' and the telling selection of the eyes. This kind of inner drama is found over and over again in Dickens: it is there at the end of this novel in Fagin's analyzed perceptions in the court (also playing a variant on the image of eyes), in the analysis of Jonas Chuzzlewit's guilty terrors, in Scrooge's nightmare of death, and in many other instances. Robert Garis, one the few critics to pay any attention to the feelings in fiction, suggests that Dickens is especially good at showing the passion of anger. To this we must add guilt and fear, or better, guilty fear. Dickens blends the extraordinary and the ordinary in his rendering of extreme states of sensation and passion. After the paragraph just quoted comes this:

And here he remained in such terror as none but he can know, trembling in every limb, and the cold sweat starting from every pore, when suddenly there arose upon the night-wind the noise of distant shouting, and the roar of voices mingled in alarm and wonder. Any sound of men in that lonely place, even though it conveyed a real cause of alarm, was something to him. He regained his strength and energy at the prospect of personal danger; and, springing to his feet, rushed into the open air.

The broad sky seemed on fire. Rising into the air with showers of sparks, and rolling one above the other, were sheets of flame, lighting the atmosphere for miles round, and driving clouds of smoke in the direction where he stood. The shouts grew louder as new voices swelled the roar, and he could hear the cry of Fire! mingled with the ringing of an alarm-bell, the fall of heavy bodies, and the crackling of flames as they twined round some new obstacle, and shot aloft as though refreshed by food. The noise increased as he looked. There were people there – men and women – light, bustle. It was like new life to him. He darted onward – straight, headlong – dashing through brier and brake, and leaping gate and fence as madly as his dog, who careered with loud and sounding bark before him.

He came upon the spot. There were half-dressed figures tearing to and fro, some endeavouring to drag the frightened horses from the stables, others driving the cattle from the yard and out-houses, and others coming laden from the burning pile, amidst a shower of falling sparks, and the tumbling down of red-hot beams. The apertures, where doors and windows stood an hour ago, disclosed a mass of raging fire; walls rocked and crumbled into the burning well; the molten lead and iron poured down, white-hot, upon the ground. Women and children shrieked, and men encouraged each other with noisy shouts and cheers. The clanking of the engine-pumps, and the spirting and hissing of the water as it fell upon the blazing wood, added to the tremendous roar. He shouted, too, till he was hoarse; and, flying from memory and himself, plunged into the thickest of the throng.

Hither and thither he dived that night: now working at the pumps, and now hurrying through the smoke and flame, but never ceasing to engage himself wherever noise and men were thickest. Up and down the ladders, upon the roofs of buildings, over floors that quaked and trembled with his weight, under the lee of falling bricks and stones, in every part of that great fire was he; but he bore a charmed life, and had neither scratch nor bruise, nor weariness nor thought, till morning dawned again, and only smoke and blackened ruins remained.

(ch. 48)

Dickens tells us that Sikes is energized at the thought of personal danger, that it is like new life, that he is escaping from memory and himself, but he also leaves much to the action's eloquence. It tells us that Sikes could only escape from one torment into another, that he needed men and women, that a delirium of action worked, but did not last. It is a perfect instance of Dickens contriving an event that despite melodramatic violence and improbability makes itself accepted because it is such a good carrier of passion. That makes it sound too static: it is, rather, a generator of passion. We see an aspect of guilt and fear; we also see the needs, sensations, and perceptions that join Sikes with common humanity. I need not labour the additional work that Dickens gets out of his action: the fire-fighting gives symbolic expression to violence, destructiveness, desperation, and ruin; Sikes needs the fire, he is also like the fire – burning, raging, rocking, and breaking.

Oliver Twist does not lack flaws; Dickens is always weak in his handling of the tender passions, and the portrayals of charity and love here are feebly articulated in comparison with the handling of fear and terror. The

38

pastoral scenes are banal. The excursus on the illness of Rose Maylie is an all-too-vivid example of the flexibility of large, loose, baggy Victorian novels, which allowed Dickens a space to indulge a private grief for his sister-in-law's death. But it achieves affective subtlety and grasps a central subject.

NICHOLAS NICKLEBY

In *Nicholas Nickleby* (1838–1839) there is a similar weakness and a similar strength, but Dickens is beginning to develop and expand his versatility in creating character. To isolate particular themes is misleading: the novel makes a devastatingly harsh and grotesque indictment of education, but this occupies a relatively small part of the action; it is concerned in many ways with theatricality and role playing, but to relate this theme to all characters and all events is to lose depth in surface. At the centre of the novel, in both typicality and emotional complexity, stands Ralph Nickleby. Like Sikes, he is an example of Dickens' imaginative capacity for creating human monsters and monstrous humans. Ralph can be seen in some lights as fabulous, in others as realistic: he is both. Dickens, like Jane Austen, creates caricatures not simply, as terms of art, but complexly, as aspects of life. Dickens postulates a human nature that is warped, hardened, drained, chilled. The simplifications of character are not properly described in terms of literary choice or literary convention, though we have to acknowledge the Victorian concern with comic and eccentric character, and Dickens' own heady oscillations from laughter to violence. The simplifications of character are present in Dickens, however, as T. A. Jackson observed long ago, because he was reflecting the reifications of society. Like all great novelists of the nineteenth century, Dickens meditates consciously and unconsciously on the key question that Henry James put in the words of Madame Merle in *The Portrait of a Lady*

(1881): 'What shall we call our 'self'? Where does it begin? Where does it end? It overflows into everything that belongs to us – and then it flows back again' (ch. 19).

Ralph Nickleby's complexity is an example of Dickens' imaginative handling of character and his awareness of nature and social shaping. We may at first sight take Ralph's detestation of Nicholas for an instinctive loathing of goodness by evil, but the novel eventually lets us know that there is a much more plausible and simple human cause in Ralph's reawakened sexual jealousy. Part of the complexity of this characterization – standing out, as it does, in an action that has few complex characters – lies in the way in which Dickens slowly unfolds causality and, with it, nature. He begins with a brief and unrevealing summary of the Nickleby family history, disclosing little about the elder brother, but Ralph is slowly revealed, as a monster who has been made monstrous by a social structure built on the values of avarice and greed. Throughout the novel Dickens lets slivers of light fall on Ralph: we are told at first that his heart has rusted and is 'only a piece of cunning mechanism, and yielding not one throb of hope, or fear, or love, or care, for any living thing,' but it turns out to be capable, after all, of one or two throbs.

Chapter 19 ends with a small incident, reminiscent of the pawned forget-me-not ring and *The Awakening Conscience*. Kate has just got into the coach after the dinner party at Ralph Nickleby's, and as the door closes, a comb falls out of her hair. Ralph picks it up and sees her face picked out in the lamplight, especially a 'lock of hair that had escaped and curled loosely over her brow.' Ralph is moved by 'some dormant train of recollection,' reminded of his dead brother's face 'with the very look it bore on some occasion of boyish grief.' Dickens then rises into the crescendo and climax: 'Ralph Nickleby, who was proof against all appeals of blood and kindred – who was steeled against every tale of sorrow and distress – staggered while he looked, and went back into his house, as a man who had seen a spirit from some world beyond the grave.'

The internal economy of Dotheboys Hall   Nicholas Nickleby
                                                Phiz

But as it happens, Dickens has already shown Ralph as a
little moved, and the earlier instance is one of those tiny
realistic touches that are worth ten of the more
melodramatic scenes from the inner life. Slightly earlier,
at the end of Ralph's dinner party, Kate is weeping, and
Dickens makes the point that Ralph is vulnerable – not
very, but slightly – because his ruling passion is for the the
moment not involved:

Ralph would have walked into any poverty-stricken debtor's
house, and pointed him out to a bailiff, though in attendance
upon a young child's death-bed, without the smallest concern,
because it would have been a matter quite in the ordinary
course of business, and the man would have been an offender

against his only code of morality. But, here was a young girl, who had done no wrong save that of coming into the world alive; who had patiently yielded to all his wishes; who had tried hard to please him – above all, who didn't owe him money – and he felt awkward and nervous.

(ch. 19)

It is moments like these that create a sense of emotional wholeness and sequence in the flat characters. They also show the human surplus, the vital remnants of nature not wholly perverted. Notice how completely unsentimental this last observation is; it even allows us a flash of contempt for Ralph, the denatured man being invoked in order to explain the surplus touch of nature. It contrasts strongly with the incident of the lock of hair in the lamplight, which belongs less to the truthful observations of psychology than to the crude melodrama of the inner life.

Nicholas Nickleby is a larger and looser novel than *Oliver Twist*, and although the concern with the making of men by society is a dominant theme, there are many facets of the action that sparkle with an independent glitter. The long and episodic novel has more scope for weakness than *Oliver Twist*, but its dangerous areas are the same. The presentation of the romantic heroine, Kate Nickleby, is often fortunately obscured by the comedy or violence of context. The febrile comic play of the Mantalinis or the sinister predatoriness of the high-life seducers compensate for what is at best a shadowy stereotype of womanly beauty and virtue. The same excess and sentimentality pump up the benevolent figure of the Cheeryble brothers: Dickens' defence of their realism by reference to their reality is singularly beside the point.

Nicholas himself, like David Copperfield, is in the direct line of descent from the heroes of the eighteenth-century adventure novels of Fielding and Smollett, which Dickens had read and admired. Dickens has David imagine himself as 'a child's Tom Jones,' and some of Dickens' other heroes can be similarly described.

Pickwick and Oliver have mythic pretensions, Nicholas has none. He is the most neutral of a line that includes David Copperfield and Pip, who become more complicated in moral and psychological life. Nicholas is a Victorian version of the eighteenth-century rogue hero, with most of the rogue removed. His personal adventures are circumscribed, but Dickens exploits his neutrality. Nicholas' blandness as a character almost passes without notice, because he is so often the observer or the object of stronger emotional action. He provides a context, for example, for the strong theatrical comedy of the Crummles family and troupe.

Dickens dedicated the novel to the great tragic actor W. C. Macready, and the assimilation of drama to narrative that began in *Sketches by Boz* becomes fully developed in a novelistic action of farce and melodrama and an exuberant criticism of theatricality in character. Nicholas provides a foil and an object for Ralph Nickleby's sharply observed moral jealousy: the emotional variety of one character throws into relief the nullity of the other, but also compensates for it. Nicholas is also a neutral point of view for presenting the most famous topical satire in the novel, that attack on the brutal Yorkshire schools which was one of the first examples of Dickens' socially effective propaganda. Comedy is often blended with pathos and grotesque horror in the characters of the Squeers family, and in some of the educational dialogue, but the Squeers' schoolroom is like an inferno, often unrelieved by humour and particularized by hideous physical detail, like Bolder's wart-covered hands, and the boys' 'foul appearance of dirt, disorder, and disease.' Dickens actually uses the words 'incipient Hell' after descriptions which show that his sense of horror works not only rhetorically but critically:

Pale and haggard faces, lank and bony figures, children with the countenances of old men, deformities with irons upon their limbs, boys of stunted growth, and others whose long meagre legs would hardly bear their stooping bodies, all crowded on the view together; there were the bleared eye, the hare-lip, the crooked foot, and every ugliness or distortion that told of unnatural aversion conceived by parents for their offspring, or of young lives which, from the earliest dawn of infancy, had been one horrible endurance of cruelty and neglect. There were little faces which should have been handsome, darkened with the scowl of sullen dogged suffering; there was childhood with the light of its eye quenched.

(ch. 8)

One of the isolated glories of *Nicholas Nickleby* reminds us of the richness of local story telling in *Pickwick Papers*. It is hard to relate Mrs. Nickleby's comic story telling to the novel's social concern, and imprecise to take it as evidence of the theatrical theme, since she has so much in common with other Dickensian narrators, like the Bagman and Mrs. Gamp. She is sufficiently stereotyped to arouse expectation, sufficiently inventive and versatile to cause surprise. Dickens, like George Eliot, if more roughly, divides characters into egoists and altruists, and Mrs. Nickleby is one of his great egocentric tellers. She constitutes a perpetual challenge to the notion of organic unity that still haunts Dickens criticism, and resembles Dickens' great villains, Fagin, Quilp, the Brasses, or Uriah Heep, in her rapturous vitality. But the vitality is not naive: Dickens is like all great storytellers in his interest in the act and art of story-telling. Mrs. Nickleby's total unawareness of communication is expressive of her self-aggrandizing intent and her sheer dottiness, itself a mark of mindlessness in a novel that takes some interest in differentiating between minds. She is comically guilty of all the narrative sins, as she rambles, forgets, stumbles, misses the point, and loses a sense of her listeners, but nourishes our delight in the zany and the absurd. Her narrative is creative, disordered, but crammed with gorgeous particulars:

'I really am very subject to colds, indeed – very subject. I had a cold once,' said Mrs. Nickleby, 'I think it was in the year eighteen hundred and seventeen; let me see, four and five are nine, and – yes, eighteen hundred and seventeen, that I thought

I should never get rid of . . . I was only cured at last by a remedy that I don't know whether you ever happened to hear of, Mr. Pluck. You have a gallon of water as hot as you can possibly bear it, with a pound of salt and six pen'orth of the finest bran, and sit with your head in it for twenty minutes every night just before going to bed; at least, I don't mean your head – your feet.

(ch. 27)

Although these anecdotes show Dickens' freedom of comic effect, they are tethered within a local context. This story, for instance, is ironically placed in a scene where the listeners are Sir Mulberry Hawk's aides, Pyke and Pluck, just as the story in the previous chapter, about the hackney coach, was told to Sir Mulberry and Lord Verisopht. Mrs. Nickleby is allowed to take off on her fine flights for our pleasure, but her narrative is brought into connection with plot. Her solipsism has dramatic consequences. Dickens is reworking the comic anecdote but with a new control.

THE OLD CURIOSITY SHOP

In 1840 Dickens began to bring out *Master Humphrey's Clock*, a weekly miscellany of fictitious papers given a tenuous unity by the device of the old clock, at once a repository and a reminder of time. The scheme was abandoned, but out of it grew *The Old Curiosity Shop*, one of his most popular and uneven novels. As in *Pickwick Papers*, the unevenness is largely one of language: the grotesque and comic parts have indivi-duality, the solemn and serious parts none. What Gerard Manley Hopkins calls 'the rehearsal' of 'self' is restricted to certain affective areas, and the restriction is especially marked in a novel where the tender emotions are so central to plot and action. Nell's adventures and feelings are very much more prolonged and active than those of Oliver, as she is dramatized in a long ordeal of living and dying. She is nearer adulthood than Oliver and is given a

Little Nell dead

The Old Curiosity Shop
G. Cattermole

whole range of moral and psychological experience which raises expectations Dickens cannot satisfy. It is hard, if not impossible, to separate conception and language: there is a correlation of weak language with certain emotional and moral areas. In the famous deathbed scene, there is stock response, strong demand for pity, no particularity, and every stop pulled out – child, nature, hearth, beauty:

She was dead. Dear, gentle, patient, noble Nell was dead. Her little bird – a poor slight thing the pressure of a finger would have crushed – was stirring nimbly in its cage; and the strong heart of its child-mistress was mute and motionless for ever.

Where were the traces of her early cares, her sufferings, and fatigues? All gone. Sorrow was dead indeed in her, but peace and perfect happiness were born; imaged in her tranquil beauty and profound repose.

And still her former self lay there, unaltered in this change.
Yes. The old fireside had smiled upon that same sweet face; it
had passed, like a dream, through haunts of misery and care.

(ch. 71)

Since Dickens depends so much on the solemn and
intense appeal to ideals of virtue, such banality of feeling
is a gross defect. It is true that some aspects of religious,
aesthetic, and domestic values are dated and counter-
productive, but this is not the central issue. When Oscar
Wilde said it took a heart of stone not to laugh at Little
Nell, he was responding to Dickens' banal language and
sentimental indulgence, two sides of the same coin of cant
appeal. It does not do to defend such simplifications on
the grounds that the characters have a mythical or
fairytale appeal. In the real fairy tale or folk tale, there is
simplicity, bareness, matter-of-factness, particularity,
and reticence. The heroes and heroines of folk tale are
unaccompanied by wholesome emotional and moral
solicitation: the reader is not held to ransom for
sympathy. Dickens is to move toward particularities of
fact and feeling in *Dombey and Son* and *Bleak House*, but
he has not yet arrived at them in *The Old Curiosity Shop*.

At the beginning the narrator notices the power of
visual objects to impress the mind:

I am not sure I should have been so thoroughly possessed by
this one subject, but for the heaps of fantastic things I had seen
huddled together in the curiosity-dealer's warehouse. These,
crowding on my mind, in connection with the child, and
gathering round her, as it were, brought her condition palpably
before me.

(ch. 1)

This rare technical and psychological comment reminds
us of particularity. Where the novel fails, there is
generalization, abstraction, banality, and nothing
palpable. Where it succeeds, in the vigorous comic
horrors of Quilp and the Brasses, Mrs. Jarvey's
waxworks, the desolate and hideous industrial imagery,
the compassionate comedy of the marchioness, Dickens is
giving us the particulars of sense and emotion, not

47

making large flamboyant gestures and stock appeal. As
Aldous Huxley says in his essay 'Vulgarity in Literature'
(1930), 'Nell's virtues are marooned, as it were, in the
midst of a boundless waste of unreality; isolated, they
fade and die. Even her sufferings and death lack
significance because of this isolation.'

BARNABY RUDGE

Out of *Master Humphrey's Clock* also came *Barnaby
Rudge*, Dickens' first historical novel, ambitious in its
research and its topicality, as he recreated the revolu-
tionary and religious struggles of the Gordon Riots
(1780) at the time of the industrial and religious unrest
and Chartist and Protestant associations of the late
1830's and early 1840's. Plot mysteries are central but too
obscurely dramatized to provide puzzle or tension. There
is very little comedy, though Dickens gives a central place
to a virulent attack on women, which dramatizes two
extremes of women's 'absurdity': the comely and
rebellious shrew Mrs. Varden, rebuked and converted
into a good wife, and the hysterical man-eating ugly
spinster, her maid Miggs. Some pressure of personal
feeling seems present in this aggressive satire, which is
compounded by the approval lavished on the stock
heroine in the high-life love story and on the arch Dolly
Varden with her homely John in the low-life romance.
Most powerful are the portraits of villainy. Dennis the
hangman is animated by a colloquial style and black
humour:

'I've heerd a eloquence on them boards – you know what
boards I mean – and have heerd a degree of mouth given to
them speeches, that they was clear as a bell, and as good as a
play. There's a pattern! And always, when a thing of this natur's
to come off, what I stand up for, is, a proper frame of mind.
Let's have a proper frame of mind, and we can go through with
it, creditable – pleasant – sociable. Whatever you do (and I
address myself, in particular, to you in the furthest), never
snivel.'

(ch. 65)

In striking contrast is the polished hypocrite, Sir John Chester, and here too the energetic particularity of character derives directly from language. Chester anticipates the devastating but amusing effrontery and hypocrisy of Skimpole in *Bleak House* and, like Dennis, is a character who is not treated humourously but created as a humourist. His son, Edward, is unparticularized in every way and speaks a banal language that registers neither feeling nor character: 'I will endeavour earnestly and patiently, if ever man did, to open some prospect for myself, and free you from the burden you fear I should become if I married one whose worth and beauty are her chief endowments.' His father is thoroughly imagined, particularized by gesture and accessory, as he moves in his seat, lays down the paper, and pares his nails with an elegant little knife, and by superciliousness of style and aggressions of irony and wit: 'You have to thank me, Ned, for being of good family; for your mother, charming person as she was, and almost broken-hearted, and so forth, as she left me, when she was prematurely compelled to become immortal – had nothing to boast of in that respect' (ch. 15).

Where Dickens has a sense of character, he has a sense of style. As is commonly observed, the pattern of character and theme is unified. Barnaby's weak brain parallels that of Lord George Gordon, and the Willett father and son parallel the Chesters. The characters take their part, personally and illustratively, in the central action of the riots, which are shown with a considerable mastery of description and detail. This formal responsiveness, however, seems less important than the political interest it conveys. Dickens' sense of compassion is present, but shadowed by a fear of social disturbance. That disturbance is dramatized in highly effective crowd scenes and satirized incisively through caricature. The ineffective Lord Mayor of London and the civic chaos are done with painfully accurate comedy, and the survey of political motive and character – loyal, disloyal, cynical, idealistic, naive, brutal, manipulative – is brilliantly imaged, for instance, in Gashford, the treacherous secretary, the well-meaning Lord George Gordon, and the parodying figure of Barnaby. In Barnaby Rudge himself, the image of the virtuous child has been transformed into that of the susceptible and pathetic fool. Sentimental by Shakespearean standards, like his predecessor Smike in *Nicholas Nickleby*, Barnaby gives Dickens a double opportunity. In this poor fool, Dickens caricatures and indicts what he saw as the exciting mindlessness of revolution, and Barnaby's central position as eponymous hero draws attention to his rhetorical function. He also gives Dickens congenial psychological material for fantasy and wildness, important in a novel that almost entirely lacks any rendering of interior life. Barnaby's dreams and madness give a release and relief that are welcome in this novel where there is no free comedy.

AMERICAN NOTES

The financial success of *American Notes* persuaded Dickens to send Martin Chuzzlewit to America. He was obviously intent on extending and intensifying his satire, which was based on social observation but stimulated by the abuse he had suffered in the American press. The results were immediate: an increase in the English sales of some 3,000, and more American abuse for the aggressive caricature and criticism. America provided him with a national emblem of self-aggrandizement.

MARTIN CHUZZLEWIT

Martin Chuzzlewit presents a coherently worked-out theme, the theme of self. The impersonations of the elder Chuzzlewit, the exiles of Martin, Mark Tapley, Tom Pinch, the attempted murder of Anthony Chuzzlewit, and the murder of Tigg Montague, the speculator and blackmailer, are all caused by selfishness or unselfishness. Selfishness is given its form of Nemesis, including Pecksniff's deceit and hubris, the punishment of Mercy in her marriage to Jonas, the ordeal of Martin in Eden, and the stern advice given to Mrs. Gamp. On the credit side there are the rewards of Tom, Ruth, John Westlock, Mark Tapley, and the young Martin. The theme expresses itself actively – apart from the content of character – in the demonstration of a change of heart and moral causality.

The important part of the action that runs right through the novel is the impersonation of old Chuzzlewit, and its consequences in the duping of Pecksniff and the exile of Martin. It provides some mystery, some irony, and some scenes that enact the humours. There is the hypocritical domestic show put on for Martin's benefit, several scenes of moral antithesis between young Martin and Tom Pinch, the splendid quarrel scene in which the predatory Chuzzlewit hypocrites fall out, the scene where old Chuzzlewit lies to Pecksniff while Pecksniff is lying to him. Such scenes are frequent at the beginning, then thin out and reappear in a conspicuous huddle toward the end when we have the revelation of Martin's trick, the exposure of Pecksniff, and the general apportionment of rewards and punishments. This one overarching piece of action does indeed overarch. It is important at the beginning and end but strays more or less out of sight for a large part of the novel, and when it does appear it is markedly unproductive of tension. There are indeed so few rising intonations of curiosity, doubt, and expectation at the beginning of the novel that it is not surprising that it was not a success as a serial; though no doubt all the other reasons that have been suggested for this relative failure – disappointment with *Barnaby Rudge*, reviewers' hostility to *American Notes*, the change to monthly publication, harshness of satire, lack of pathetic children and deaths – may also be important. But the striking difference between this novel and almost all Dickens' others is this absence of initial tension. Incident and human emotional centre are both present, for instance, in the death of Mrs. Dombey, the mystery of Esther's birth, Pip's encounter with Magwitch, the first river scene in *Our Mutual Friend*. Sometimes the incident alone is arresting, as in the workhouse scene in the first chapter of *Oliver Twist*. Sometimes the introductory scene is symbolic, as in *Bleak House* and *Little Dorrit*. But in all these novels we also move swiftly forward to a strong human identification. Leaving aside the tiresome exercise in sarcasm that is the prelude to *Martin Chuzzlewit*, there is no exciting incident in the early chapters. There are few strongly exciting situations anywhere in the novel, apart from Martin's trip to Eden and the criminal career of Jonas Chuzzlewit, and neither of these sources of tension is anticipated by any early trailers.

The human centre is missing too: the most interesting and conspicuous character is Pecksniff, one of Dickens' most brilliant and hideous comic stereotypes. Martin is too neutral and uninteresting, and is scarcely ever seen from the inside until his crisis of conversion. The one character whose emotions are dramatized with any strength is Tom Pinch, and he is not only a grossly sentimental figure but is also given practically nothing to do. In these three characters, as they appear, there seems to be no potentiality for tense action or emotional identification; but the big wasted opportunity is in the conflict and impersonation of old Martin. This impersonation is neither prominent nor productive of mystery, plot influence, or dramatic irony. Boffin's assumed humour in *Our Mutual Friend* is motivated, influential, and provides a heightened moral symbol of the prevailing evil in the novel. Martin's impersonation is weakly motivated and has barely more than a concluding pantomimic resolution in action.

If the moral content does not terminate in action, what makes the incident of the early parts of the novel? There are brilliant comic scenes with lively satire, linguistic humour, and farce, but although these scenes usually have thematic relevance, they seldom move beyond a self-contained action that raises no questions and leaves no disturbing loose ends. There is some attempt at the moral conflict that in other novels produces its tension, in personal relationships that form a moral antithesis (Nicholas and Smike, Dombey and Florence, Hexam and Lizzie), but the moral antithesis in *Martin Chuzzlewit* is thin and formal. There is the moral opposition of old Martin and Pecksniff, and of young Martin with Tom Pinch and Mark Tapley. None of these morally significant pairs is shown in the tension of personal relations: there is no human antagonism, or love, or fear, or any of the conflicting emotions that mark the relations of Oliver and Fagin, or Pip and Magwitch, or Florence and Dombey, where the moral antithesis is complex in each case and admits of change. The only parts of *Chuzzlewit* that show a personal as well as a moral conflict are either presented offstage in exposition, like the relationship between Martin and his grandfather, or are not explored for moral antithesis. Mary's relation to the sadistic Jonas, with its pleas and cries on behalf of outraged sacred womanhood, or the relation of Mary Graham to Pecksniff in his role of repulsive furtive lecher, are not moving as moral demonstrations.

These two structures of character bring out the mixture of styles and powers in this novel. Mercy is translated from her satiric and comic role into the area of romantic melodrama, where a different treatment is applied in response to a new affective demand. Dickens fails to create any continuity of character, simply grafting a new set of characteristics onto an old one, interestingly shifting the name from Merry to Mercy. In David Copperfield and Betsey Trotwood, he succeeds in integrating comic and serious functions, but in *Martin Chuzzlewit* he can only manage one register at a time. When the new Mercy is created, there is another disjunction because Dickens fails to handle the experiences of love and suffering but manages excellently with those of guilt and criminal fear. Mercy fails to create pity, but Jonas creates that blend of horrified expectation and surprise that Dickens so powerfully manipulated as early as *Oliver Twist*. Similarly Mary Graham's appeal as victim is null compared with Pecksniff's as grotesque seducer. There are, and remain, certain emotions that Dickens fails to imagine: the weak language used for Mary and Mercy contrasts with the bizarre and novel language used for Pecksniff and Jonas. Dickens is not alone among great writers in this unevenness of imagination. Ben Jonson's virtuous characters in *Volpone* are feebly articulated compared with those conceived as strong grotesques, and both Thackeray and George Eliot reveal spots of commonness in certain areas of pathos and admiration. The reasons for such inequalities are a matter of speculation: the artistic experience suggests that certain emotions are congenial and others not, but such congeniality is probably in part personal and in part social. Dickens and Thackeray, for instance, are what may be carefully called typically Victorian in their occasional stereotyping of womanly virtue, but Thackeray is a more radical analyst of the duplicities and mutabilities of what we call love than is Dickens.

Martin Chuzzlewit, then, succeeds in harsh and exuberant satire, in the manipulation of an externally and internally exciting crime story, and in the creation of great comic characters, such as Pecksniff and Mrs. Gamp. Mrs. Gamp is Mrs. Nickleby's successor, a powerful and disturbing teller of tales, providing a series of marvellously comic anecdotes that do much more than entertain, being fully expressive of character and playing a surprising part in the plot. Both Mrs. Gamp and Mrs. Harris play a cunningly devised part in the revelation scene and its listener's response, but Mrs. Gamp's last story forms a fine example of Dickens' not altogether successful attempt to integrate effects:

'Which, Mr. Chuzzlewit,' she said, 'is well beknown to Mrs. Harris as has one sweet infant (though she *do* not wish it known) in her own family by the mother's side, kep' in spirits in a bottle; and that sweet babe she see at Greenwich Fair, a-travelling in company with the pink-eyed lady, Prooshan dwarf, and livin' skelinton, which judge her feelins when the barrel organ played, and she was showed her own dear sister's child, the same not being expected from the outside picter, where it was painted quite contrairy in a livin' state, a many sizes larger, and performing beautiful upon the Arp, which never did that dear child know or do: since breathe it never did, to speak on, in this wale! And Mrs. Harris, Mr. Chuzzlewit, has knowed me many year, and can give you information that the lady which is widdered can't do better and may do worse, than let me wait upon her, which I hope to do. Permittin' the sweet faces as I see afore me.'

(ch. 52)

There is a falling off, as old Martin addresses his didactic speech to 'the astonished Mrs. Gamp,' 'hinting at the expediency of a little less liquor, and a little more regard for her patients, and perhaps a trifle of additional honesty.' Mrs. Gamp is an impermeable and incorrigible character – unlike young Martin and Mark Tapley – and the final exchange shows the insulation of modes and styles and Dickens' awareness of a need to bring them closer together.

A CHRISTMAS CAROL

In *A Christmas Carol* Scrooge sees his own image in the most literal fashion, moving back in time and confronting himself at different stages in his process of deterioration. There is his old self, the child, loving and innocent opposite of the unloving old sophist. There is the transitional self, committed to loveless rationalism, but still holding some few warm contacts with the past. There is his mirror image, the present self, who echoes his own words and sentiments but in a context newly charged with feeling. The doubles, like the ghosts, are all potent in different ways, and indeed the ghosts are not only aspects of Christmas but also aspects of Scrooge: his past, his present, and his suggestive anonymous future. The return to childhood restores him to the first springs of love in a way reminiscent of Wordsworth and George Eliot; the personal past is a tradition that can keep alive the feeling child, father of the rational man. It also gives a brief glimpse of the deprived and isolated child. Instead of a recognition of causality – though that is obliquely present – we have in Scrooge himself the equally effective stirring of love and pity. He sees his sister, rather as Silas Marner remembers his sister after he first sees Eppie, and the link is made with old affection and old sorrow. He 'feels pity for his former self' and the pity brings with it the first movement of imaginative self-criticism. He identifies his old sorrow with sorrow outside himself: 'There was a boy singing a Christmas Carol at my door last night. I should like to have given him something: that's all' (stave 2). This is of course the carol that gives the story its name, and also its theme: 'God bless you, merry gentlemen, may nothing you dismay.' Scrooge threatens the boy with his ruler, rejects the blessing, and Christmas brings him a strong but salutary dismay.

The Ghost of Christmas Past acts as devil's advocate, and his timing is admirable. Scrooge is identifying himself with his former self at Fezziwig's ball: 'His heart and soul were in the scene, and with his former self. He corroborated everything, remembered everything, enjoyed everything, and underwent the strangest agitation' (stave 2). The Ghost pours cold water on the apprentices' gratitude: 'A smaller matter... to make these silly folks so full of gratitude... He has spent but a few pounds of your mortal money: three or four perhaps'. So Scrooge is forced to defend the generous spirit, heated by the remark, and speaking unconsciously like his former, not his latter, self: 'The happiness he gives, is quite as great as if it cost a fortune.' Then he suddenly remembers his present self, and gently urged by his ghostly analyst, moves toward self-criticism. The process is continued by the Ghost, in stave 3, who answers Scrooge's question about Tiny Tim: 'If he be like to die, he had better do it, and decrease the surplus population.'

56

Marley's Ghost

A Christmas Carol
J. Leech

When Scrooge is overcome 'with penitence and grief' at his own words, the Ghost comes in quickly with the grave rebuke: 'Forbear that wicked cant until you have discovered What the surplus is, and Where it is.' The Ghost employs the same mimicry when he shows the terrible children, Want and Ignorance. Scrooge's newborn horror, like his compassion, is answered by his own words: 'Are there no prisons? ... Are there no work-houses?' This technique of exact quotation comes decorously enough in the Christmas present, rubbing Scrooge's nose in his very recent refusal to give to the portly gentleman. The arguments for charity were also presented in personification ('Want is keenly felt, and Abundance rejoices') but they have to be acted out for the unimaginative man, forcing him to walk through the crowds and see them composed not of ciphers but of individuals. All the elements in this brief masque are appropriate. They show to the hardened man the need and love in his own past; they show to the old killjoy his dead capacity for joy. Having indicated causality and change, the show ends with a memento mori, cold, solitary, and repulsive, in the new perspective of feeling. Effective argument is implied in the dramatic reclamation by love and fear, and we are left with the urgent question – Is reclamation still possible?, which makes the modulation from nightmare to fantasy. The fantasy has a realistic suggestion of hypnotic therapy.

DOMBEY AND SON

One might suggest that the poise and control of fable and feeling in *A Christmas Carol* constitute a turning point in Dickens' development. The novels that follow are all great novels, with the exception of *A Tale of Two Cities*. They show a balance of the various Dickensian interests – in social satire, love story, psychological and moral fable, and plot mystery. Linguistic variety and brilliance are more sustained, and Dickens has learned to carry into the serious style the figurative brilliance that was once reserved for his comic effects. The tautness of *A Christmas Carol*, outstanding in all five of the Christmas books written between 1843 and 1848, may well have helped to break down the barriers that previously existed between his different stylistic registers of thinking and feeling.

Dombey and Son also benefits from Dickens' total social commitment in the Christmas books and returns him wholeheartedly to criticism of the unjust and acquisitive society. Dombey embodies pride, but it is sharply and diagnostically shown as a capitalistic pride, the paternal pride acting in the interest of transactional possessiveness and expansion. The novel also shows Dickens' most impressive use of his affective medium.

The symbolic use of that great Victorian symbol, the railway, shows Dickens' fusion of social and psychological drama. The railway is connected with the whole industrial scene of the novel, and we see it grow, make changes, employ real people. Dickens makes quite plain the gap between the railway's symbolic rendering of Dombey and its larger life. Dickens picks up, for instance, the violence of its noise, the iron way, and its speed. He also makes it quite plain that Dombey's sensations and feelings are selecting the symbolic points, that the train's journey, landscape, and effects are not wholly or simply as Dombey interprets them: 'He found no pleasure or relief in the journey. Tortured by these thoughts he carried monotony with him, through the rushing landscape, and hurried headlong, not through a rich and varied country, but a wilderness of blighted plans and gnawing jealousies' (ch. 20). Dombey chooses the dark, but there exists the light; there is a wilderness without like the wilderness within, but there are also richness and variety. When Dombey moves into the industrial horrors, Dickens makes explicit what was formerly implicit:

There are dark pools of water, muddy lanes, and miserable habitations far below. There are jagged walls and falling houses close at hand, and through the battered roofs and broken windows, wretched rooms are seen, where want and fever hide themselves in many wretched shapes, while smoke and crowded gables, and distorted chimneys, and deformity of brick and water penning up deformity of mind and body, choke the murky distance. As Mr. Dombey looks out of his carriage window, it is never in his thoughts that the monster who has brought him there has let the light of day in on these things: not made or caused them.

(ch. 20)

The railway links Dombey with Carker. Carker is afraid of death, and throughout the description of his flight, Dickens incorporates the unknown object of the fear into the fear itself. Carker feels alienated chiefly because he has been mortified and hit where he felt most confident, in his sexual vanity. He also feels alienated because he is in a foreign country. And Dickens makes his very self-consciousness increase the feeling of dissociation in a perceptive stroke: 'The dread of being hunted in a strange remote place, where the laws might not protect him – the novelty of the feeling that it was strange and remote, originating in his being left alone so suddenly amid the ruins of his plans' (ch. 55). Like Sikes, the character opens out, largely by means of acutely rendered new feeling. The whole episode is also an inner melodrama of violent fear and desperate turmoil of feeling – the violence is right for Carker, as it was for Sikes, and once more keeps sensational action and passion on the highroad of human experience. This symbolism of feelings is more subtle than anything in *Oliver Twist*. Pre-echo replaces explicit anticipation, sensation is excitingly in advance of explication. We do not understand why Carker feels a rush, hears a bell, and is aware of a sweep of 'something through the air' until he comes to be killed by the train, and symbol is discovered at the moment of climax. The imagery of the river and the wild waves is assertive in its recurrences, but Dickens is slowly learning the effectiveness of suggestion. As so often, his strengths and weaknesses are close neighbours. The exaggerated unconventional language of the serious loves in *Martin Chuzzlewit* was accompanied by the parody of amorous intensity and hyperbole in the exclamations and personifications in Moddle's style. One of the difficulties of judging Dickens' language of feeling lies in such intimate mingling of success and failure, so conspicuous in *Dombey and Son*.

The account of Paul's death, for instance, concludes with an intense appeal to stock response, through a generalized imagery, a series of exclamations, and the climactic invocation of childhood, the garden of Eden, and immortality. As so often, Dickens accumulates in the hope of intensifying, but diffuses and stereotypes:

The golden ripple on the wall came back again, and nothing else stirred in the room. The old, old fashion! The fashion that came in with our first garments, and will last unchanged until our race has run its course, and the wide firmament is rolled up like a scroll. The old, old fashion – Death!

Oh thank GOD, all who see it, for that older fashion yet, of Immortality! And look upon us, angels, of young children, with regards not quite estranged, when the swift river bears us to the ocean!

(ch. 16)

Earlier in this chapter, Dickens is writing with a constant attention to emotional particulars, recording the experience of pain and death from the inside, solidifying and realizing the imagery of the wild waves through the drama of the dying child's imagination:

When the sunbeams struck into his room through the rustling blinds, and quivered on the opposite wall like golden water, he knew that evening was coming on, and that the sky was red and beautiful. As the reflection died away, and a gloom went creeping up the wall, he watched it deepen, deepen into night. Then he thought how the long streets were dotted with lamps, and how the peaceful stars were shining overhead. His fancy had a strange tendency to wander to the river, which he knew was flowing through the great city; and now he thought how black it was, and how deep it would look, reflecting the hosts of stars – and more than all, how steadily it rolled away to meet the sea.

As it grew later in the night, and footsteps in the street became so rare that he could hear them coming, count them as they passed, and lose them in the hollow distance, he would lie and watch the many-coloured ring about the candle, and wait patiently for day. His only trouble was, the swift and rapid river. He felt forced, sometimes, to try to stop it – to stem it with his childish hands – or choke its way with sand – and when he saw it coming on, resistless, he cried out! But a word from Florence, who was always at his side, restored him to himself; and leaning his poor head upon her breast, he told Floy of his dream, and smiled.

(ch. 16)

Dickens' handling of feeling moves between these opposites, of generalization and particularity. The incisive account in which the river is physically and socially actualized, then vividly used as an emotional symbol of dying, in the description of panic and passivity, lapses into that concluding flourish at the end of the chapter.

A similarly teasing combination of effects marks the treatment of Edith Dombey, another of the novel's triumphs. Edith is one of Dickens' most subtle portraits of a woman, psychologically and socially imagined with zest, thoroughness, and precision. The novel's indictment of the patriarchal assumptions of Victorian capitalism depends largely on this piece of characterization, since Florence Dombey – the commercially invisible 'daughter' – is conceived too simply and prettily in terms of the angelic child, scarcely endorsing, let alone dramatizing, the feminist implications so radically if erratically present in this novel. Dickens' rejection of capitalist inheritance of power represents a brilliant insight into the nature of sexual politics, but it is not sustained in all the ramifications of character and action. Perhaps nowhere else – with the possible exception of the treatment of Louisa in *Hard Times* – does Dickens make such a rejection of patriarchy as he does through Edith's sense of the market and its values, her doomed and modern attempt to talk to her husband about the survival of relationship, and her highly economical sexual and social revenge on the exploitations of both husband and seducer.

The analysis and criticism, central in the very title of the novel, is supported by scenic particulars, as in the scene in Edith's boudoir (chapter 40), where the deliberate disarray of clothing and ornament image a cosmetic flouting of the conventions she has so lucidly recognized. But her language and behaviour are conceived in a way that is often stagey and banal:

It was that of a lady, elegantly dressed and very handsome, whose dark proud eyes were fixed upon the ground, and in whom some passion or struggle was raging. For as she sat looking down, she held a corner of her under lip within her mouth, her bosom heaved, her nostril quivered, her head trembled, indignant tears were on her cheek, and her foot was set upon the moss as though she would have crushed it into nothing.

(ch. 27)

Dickens' strengths and weaknesses are sometimes juxtaposed, sometimes closely interwoven. This unevenness takes a promising form in *Dombey and Son*. In *Pickwick* and even in *Martin Chuzzlewit*, banality or feebleness were separated from originality and power, but in *Dombey and Son* weaknesses and strengths tend to be married. Dickens can use stagey dialogue or description to embody subtle insights into character and society: it is no longer possible to relate weakness of style to weakness of idea. Such mingling of effects may trouble the critic, but it is productive. The deathbed of Jo, in *Bleak House*, in many ways close to the rituals and images of feeling in the deathbed of Paul, shows the effective crossing of particularity with generalization.

DAVID COPPERFIELD

Like *Dombey and Son*, *David Copperfield* belongs to the maturity of Dickens' art. There is less explicit social criticism in this novel than in the other writing; his eye was on his own domestic and spiritual adventures, not on social injustice. Being the man he was, seeing his own life necessarily involved some social criticism, but this emerges implicitly and often unconsciously. There are some exceptions. The book contains some hard nuggets of topical concern, usually extractable and conspicuous: the plea for prostitutes and their reclaim, the satire on the law, the criticism of model prisons, the interest in emigration. These mostly appear as tractlike forms within the continuum of the novel, not digressions but certainly statements in a different mode. We may feel that the treatment of Emily's seduction suffers from being part of a generalized case about fallen women, but we are likely to applaud the formalized little coda about prison reform, which allows the three villains to take a final bow and creates a new piece of satirical irony. These embedded tracts are few. More typical and more interesting is the revelation of Dickens' implicit social attitudes, often remaining well below the conscious level of criticism.

In Dickens' other study of psychological growth, *Great Expectations*, the psychological concerns are socially expressive: Pip's humiliations, ambitions, illusions, snobbishness, gentlemanliness, and fall and rise are all recognizable social symbols. The novel is at once a portrait of an individual character and a strong generalization. In *David Copperfield*, because Dickens is close to his hero and in a position where he found it hard to be distanced and objective, the relation of psychology to social expression is markedly different. David often reveals – or rather betrays – Victorian limitations that the author does not see but which the modern reader certainly does. David's dissatisfaction with Dora's housekeeping, for instance, is very plainly characteristic of both his sex and age, an expectation and a need that it never occurs to him to question or criticize. Dickens takes very great pains to show David's painful attempts, after intolerant and demanding mistakes, to accept Dora as she is, and the tolerance and compromise are clearly meant to be seen as meritorious. In a sense they are, but modern readers will set aside the limited assumption that every man deserves a good housekeeper, and sympathize with the undated and moving residue – David's difficult decision to accept another human being for what she is, which is not what he wants or needs.

Dickens makes David's observation and sensibility act as a sensitive register for the novel's several actions. At times the response is unsurprising, but at others it is interestingly marked, as on the occasion when Dickens gives the last word to Uriah Heep after David has observed, rather priggishly and very inaccurately, that 'greed and cunning' always 'over-reach themselves. It is as certain as death.' Heep replies:

'Or as certain as they used to teach at school (the same school where I picked up so much umbleness), from nine o'clock to eleven, that labour was a curse; and from eleven o'clock to one, that it was a blessing and a cheerfulness, and a dignity, and I don't know what all, eh?' said he with a sneer. 'You preach about as consistent as they did. Won't umbleness go down?'
(ch. 52)

Since the novel ends with umbleness going down splendidly, albeit in prison, this riposte seems to mark a rare division between Dickens and David. It certainly marks Dickens' imaginative recognition of the social significance of Heep and the socially determined nature of the ethics of industry. Dickens is not perhaps entirely behind the comment, for he does use his art to celebrate the certainty of vice's downfall, and he does elsewhere preach the blessedness and dignity of labour pretty loudly, but the passage marks a fruitful uncertainty, a movement of the critical imagination beyond those historical limitations that operated on it.

Critics such as Gwendolyn Needham and Edgar Johnson have praised *David Copperfield* for its powers of thematic unification and control of idea. It has also been praised for its coherent analysis of 'the undisciplined heart,' the phrase in which Annie Strong sums up her youthful, irrational, and amoral feeling, and which stirs David to self-recognition and diagnosis. Almost every character, problem, and episode can be seen as an illustration of this theme. What I want to question is that the idea and its ramifications are sources of strength. G. K. Chesterton, whose criticism combines effusiveness with much insight, said that Dickens' characters were often implausible but still possessed the power to shake us profoundly. I believe that it is not so much the explicit moral and psychological study of the heart and its discipline that gives *David Copperfield* its strength and its vitality, as certain intense local shafts that strike deep as insights and revelations.

Once David sees that his heart is undisciplined, the path ahead is fairly smooth and straight, and Dickens, here as elsewhere, illustrates the moral and psychological fallacy of identifying diagnosis with remedy. Once Martin Chuzzlewit, Scrooge, David, and Pip arrive at self-knowledge, they proceed to improvement and conversion. The actual concept of the disciplined heart seems crude and owes much to the impression made on us by another and easier kind of discipline, the discipline of action. We see David's grit and professional industry emerging from the ordeal set him by Betsey Trotwood, his fairy godmother; and by a kind of sideways shift, we may well ignore the absence of much dramatic evidence for the emotional discipline that Annie and David tell of, but do not show, in their change of heart. Annie's narrative is a summary of action and feeling, made in retrospect when she confesses to her husband. David's narrative is addressed to the reader. We are meant to feel and approve David's attempts to discipline his own demands for comfort, rational companionship, and a profound love, and to accept the deficiencies of Dora and of his marriage. Behind the pages of narrative lie Dickens' own hard and fatigued attempts to live with his own marriage, but the toughness and wryness of this experience of accepting uncomfortable life remain largely unrealized and unarticulated.

The psychological interest is erratic, appearing in spots rather than stretches, especially once we follow David into the adult world, but it is arrestingly present. David tells Dora that he has been trying to change her, has seen his error, and has decided not 'to try any more.' Dora's response is one of the many details that make her character interesting:

'It's better for me to be stupid than uncomfortable, isn't it?' said Dora.
    'Better to be naturally Dora than anything else in the world.'
    'In the world! Ah Doady, it's a large place!'

(ch. 48)

One moment like this is more delicate and moving than all the loudly whispered hints about her last talk with Agnes.

David Copperfield has a vitality that possesses comic and serious dimensions. The same is true of the comic characters. In this novel, the jokes do not explode to leave no trace. When Micawber speaks, the style is the man:

'Under the impression,' said Mr. Micawber, 'that your peregrinations in this metropolis have not as yet been extensive, and that you might have some difficulty in penetrating the arcana of the Modern Babylon in the direction of the City Road—in short,' said Mr. Micawber, in another burst of confidence, 'that you might lose yourself – I shall be happy to call this evening, and install you in the knowledge of the nearest way.'

(ch. 11)

Micawber's celebrated 'in short' does not merely show up the inflation and grandiose circumlocution of his grand flights, but cuts them short and modifies their grandiosity. The hollow men in Dickens, like Pecksniff and Chadband, irritate the reader into deflating and translating their flights; Micawber is given the ability to deflate himself, and the stylistic deflation that follows the 'in short' signals the descent to practical matters. The reader who properly attends to the style is not too startled at Micawber's final triumphs. The comedy here,

Mr. Micawber delivers some valedictory remarks   David Copperfield
                                                                    Phiz

as in other characters, is subtly deceptive and subtly
revealing. The reader has to learn, with David to see
beneath the comic simplifications, to learn, for instance,
that Mrs. Micawber's elasticity is not ludicrous, but
guarantees her much-vaunted but genuine constancy, or
that Betsey Trotwood's comic spinsterishness is neither
comic nor simple. Dickens is learning to use comedy not
simply for farce and satire, but most originally to create
surface effects and to trip us into feeling the depths
beneath. His apparently self-contained jokes and his
apparently static caricatures are dynamic and complex.

This kind of comedy is appropriately used in a novel of
memory, a novel that explores the past, re-enacts it, and
explores its meanings. The past sensations and feelings
are presented as things remembered, and the effect of the
double vision of David the past child and David the man
in the present works in the same way as the comic
duplicity. The rhythm of the novel depends largely on the
relation between the time past and present, a relation that
is made very emphatic in the several 'retrospects' where,
by a fine stroke of linguistic imagination, Dickens uses

the present tense to express what is most visibly presented as the rapid passing of time in the past, a present tense that speaks with a sad and faintly mocking voice of what was vivid and now has faded, a perfect vehicle for the ironies of nostalgic remembering, reliving, questioning, and burying:

Next day, too, when we all go in a flock to see the house – our house – Dora's and mine – I am quite unable to regard myself as its master. I seem to be there, by permission of somebody else. I half expect the real master to come home presently, and say he is glad to see me. Such a beautiful little house as it is, with everything so bright and new; with the flowers on the carpets looking as if freshly gathered, and the green leaves on the paper as if they had just come out; with the spotless muslin curtains, and the blushing rose-coloured furniture, and Dora's garden hat with the blue ribbon – do I remember, now, how I loved her in such another hat when I first knew her! – already hanging on its little peg; the guitar-case quite at home on its heels in a corner; and everybody tumbling over Jip's pagoda, which is much too big for the establishment.

(ch. 43)

Some of the most complex writing, which blends comedy and pathos, is in these passages, and it is in them that the powerfully articulated themes of mutability and memory are expressed. *David Copperfield* is a novel of 'the silent gliding on . . . of existence,' the memory of 'the unseen, unfelt progress of . . . life,' 'of the river,' and 'the journey.' The gliding is halted, the progress held up, the river stopped, and the journey interrupted, in four great punctuating chapters, placed arrestingly at the ends of instalments, where the theme becomes explicit, the narrative summary conveniently made, and the sensations of memory movingly created out of that 'historic present' that uses the language of time present to dramatize time past and delicately fuses and defines layers of experience. It is the unity of feeling emphasized by Schlegel and Coleridge to replace the rigidities of neoclassical concepts of form that seems most appropriately invoked to describe the structure, the subject, and the appeal of *David Copperfield*.

Bleak House was published in monthly parts, beginning in March 1852. It is one of the most thoroughly studied of Dickens' novels. Scholars have collated the fiction with the facts of history and concluded that this is a highly topical novel, in its Carlylean symbolism of fire and fog, and all its documentary materials. 'Documentary' is a misleading word: Dickens was a novelist, not only a reporter. He took such contemporary events and problems as the Manning case (which was the source for the murder of Tulkinghorn), the charitable efforts of Mrs. Chisholm's Family Colonisation Society, the Oxford Movement (violently and irreverently parodied in Mrs. Pardiggle and her unfortunate sons), scandals about sanitation and cholera, and the criticisms of Chancery, and reinvented them for his novel. By his own reassembly of these materials, he revealed his social diagnosis. John Carey has discussed Dickens' ambivalence and inconsistency in moral attitude, but *Bleak House* is lucid and consistent. Chancery and a great house and the brickmakers and the frightful slums of Tom-All-Alone's are inextricably joined: rank, wealth, and ease are responsible for ignorance, poverty, and pain. And if the reason will not see and accept such connections, the body will – the disease that does not know its place acts as a violent physiological metaphor for the oneness of the body politic. The fog is commonly celebrated as the controlling image of the novel, but it is really only one instance and aspect of the bleakness – cold, wet, and filthy – announced in the title. The house of England does not shelter its citizens from cruel weathers. Cold, wet, fog, and dirt are sensed as presences throughout a novel that not only makes us laugh, cry, and wait, as Dickens advised Wilkie Collins a novel should, but also makes us feel and smell.

From the very beginning of the novel, with its verbless bird's-eye view of the Thames and London, our senses are agitated. The fog's chill and blur are felt and seen – and,

Tom-all-alone's

Bleak House
Phiz

indeed, the beginning of the novel would be thin and allegorical if this were not so, for most of the equations and interpretations of the setting drawn by the critics are explicitly announced by Dickens himself. Some readers have felt Dickens' explicitness an irritant: he leaves little to be inferred, but puts the case at the top of his voice, repeats it in capital letters, and then adds an extra gloss in a footnote. These novels were read to groups of illiterates as Thackeray's and George Eliot's never were, and much can be forgiven a writer whose sympathy and entertainment have reached so many people. We move through the novel, feeling fog, damp, filth, and slime, and then, when the sensations of revulsion are held up by Esther's orderly housekeeping or Chadband's gluttonous delight, we feel the impact of the interruption. Dickens animates his simple and schematic symbol, and involves us in a close and concrete relation with places, events, and characters. As with his Fat Boy in *Pickwick*, he wants to make our flesh creep by the contaminating exposures of *Bleak House*.

He moves us through disgust and pity, but also through comedy. Most of it is strongly satirical. Mrs. Jellyby, Mr. Turveydrop, the Pardiggles, Chadband, and Harold Skimpole are contemptuously ridiculed instances of heartless and complacent survivals among so many victims. The character of Mrs. Bayham Badger is the nearest we get to a comedy in which criticism is subdued by delight: 'Mrs. Badger has been married to three husbands – two of them highly distinguished men,' said Mr. Badger, summing up the facts; 'and, each time, upon the twenty-first of March at Eleven in the forenoon!' (ch. 13). This has the old wild touch of superfluous detail; though Mrs. Badger is a type of self-isolated complacency and survival, and her best scene is carefully placed before the passage revealing the love of Ada and Richard; it has a gaiety that is rare in this dark novel. The grimness of satire is sustained in the rhetoric and language of the omniscient narrator who shares the story-telling with Esther. The language used is often hortatory, even forensic. The reader is addressed and pressed, often in the manner of a prosecuting counsel, judge, or interrogator persuading, accusing, questioning, informing, summing up. The range of tone and feeling in this cross-examination is considerable. There is dry irony: 'Mr. Vholes is a very respectable man. He is allowed by the greater attorneys who have made good fortunes, or are making them, to be a most respectable man'; and acid astringency: 'The one great principle of the English law is, to make business for itself.' The voice can shed both dryness and irony in passionate vituperation, as when the present tense gives up transitive verbs in despair on the occasion of Jo's death: 'Dead, your Majesty. Dead, my lords and gentlemen. Dead, Right Reverends and Wrong Reverends of every order. Dead, men and women, born with Heavenly compassion in your hearts. And dying thus around us every day' (ch. 47).

The stark descriptions and direct address of this threnody are of course contrasted with the placid tones of Esther's narrative. One of Esther's many disadvantages as narrator/heroine is her total lack of irony or humour, a disadvantage she shares with other virtuous models in Dickens and George Eliot, but which is here peculiarly distinct and limiting, because she is a story-teller contrasted with the flexibility and force of the other narrator. Dickens is making an experiment in narrative structure (the best account of this can be found in W. J. Harvey's essay in *Dickens and the Twentieth Century*). We move from the limited vision and feeling of Esther to the larger, darker vision whose detachment is underlined by the present tense that bleakly records the way things are. The detachment has both passion and judgment, and is rather like the detachment one would expect of a recording angel. The division between the two narratives makes particularly plain that awkward separation between the optimistic record of the individual heart and the black record of the social historian.

Esther's story shows the energy of virtue and its final happy success; the social record shows the energy of destructive injustice. We are left with the constructiveness of the good housekeeper and the good doctor, rewarded with each other, cozily settled in their rustic version of 'Bleak House,' whose 'doll's rooms' strike some readers as an impropriety after Tom-All-Alone's. Dickens does disturb the final harmony with the discords of Caddy's deaf-and-dumb child and Ada's mourning, but the strongest chords are those expressing peace, beauty restored, pain soothed, virtue recognized, energy activated, the wind never in the east. Dickens does not make his final passages ironical, and we drop down from the powerful indictment to this weak doll's-house reassurance. It is not only that Dickens tends to conventionalize his ending, but perhaps that his mind was divided. He found it possible to feel boundless hope in the human heart, little in societies and institutions. *Bleak House* suggests that as soon as generous impulse becomes institutionalized charity, it kills the love of individuals by individuals. So it is understandable, if depressing, to find that the conclusion of the novel seems so congratulatory. The reconciliation is too tiny, too unrepresentative, to emerge from this novel. The sense of its restriction is increased by Esther's own unreality: if there is indeed hope to be found in human hearts, let them be more complex and more eroded by experience than Miss Summerson's. Her symbolic name and fairy-tale associations with Dame Durden and the rest do not make her a character with genuine mythological weight, but senti-mentalize good works by excessive solicitude, admiration, and complacency. Some of the responses that the author demands for the heroine are precluded by her role as ostentatiously modest narrator. We can only be glad that it was David and not Agnes who told the story of *David Copperfield*.

In the next few novels Dickens takes pains to avoid any suggestion of an easy solution. *Hard Times, Little Dorrit, A Tale of Two Cities*, and *Great Expectations* limit their concluding demands on the reader and do not expect us to settle down and see everything and everyone as now prospering after all that pain. The sense of reality begins in *Hard Times* with a toughening of moral humours in the two chief women characters. Sissy Jupe is a more subdued type of womanly virtue than Esther, and we are asked to concentrate not on Sissy but on Louisa, a psychologically realistic character who does not tax our credulity or our faith. Like Edith Dombey, to whom she is related, Louisa is a case of repressed passion and vision. She sees the highest, but pride, self-contempt, and doubt drive her into following the lowest. She perversely represses her capacity for virtue and tries to act out the utilitarian disregard for feeling that her education has held up as a model. She is also moved by her love for her brother and does not follow Edith's earlier course of punishing herself and her male aggressors, and is indeed moved by Harthouse (and he by her and by Sissy) as Edith never is by Carker. Harthouse is a less stagey and a more compressed version of Carker, a study in perverted ennui, who is a sketch for Eugene Wrayburn. Louisa is also exposed to experience not simply as a victim, like Esther Summerson, but as a susceptible and malleable human being who has a capacity for damnation.

Though the treatment of the working-class characters and industrial problems is sentimental and crass, the virtue of *Hard Times* lies in a new kind of truthfulness about social conditioning of character. We do not find, as in *Bleak House*, the anatomy of destructiveness followed by a small-scale model of construction. The humours of the self-made man in Bounderby, and of the convertible utilitarian in Gradgrind, are incisive and spirited, very much in the manner of those Jonsonian humours whose very narrowness produces a pressure of vitality. The presentation of the circus with its symbols of pastime, joy, and goodhearted sleaziness is effective within the limits of the fable and, in spite of its embarrassing lisping innocence, responds adequately enough to the counter-symbol of the fact-choked and fact-choking schoolroom. The novel lacks a proper adult equivalent for the imaginative and sensual life denied by Gradgrind, but so much of the focus is on the child's education that this passes almost without notice. That it does not escape entirely without notice is perhaps a tribute to the delineation of passion, repression and conflict in Louisa. Dickens cannot really be said to explore her inner life, but he manages very skilfully, as with Dombey, to imply it.

Louisa does not go right down to the bottom of Mrs. Sparsit's gloatingly imagined moral staircase, but her redemption is treated with some sternness, and there is no falsely triumphant climax. The anatomy of a heartless education and heartless industrialism, linked by the criterion of efficiency, concludes with no more than a sad and sober appraisal:

Herself again a wife – a mother – lovingly watchful of her children, ever careful that they should have a childhood of the mind no less than a childhood of the body, as knowing it to be even a more beautiful thing, and a possession, any hoarded scrap of which, is a blessing and happiness to the wisest? Did Louisa see this? Such a thing was never to be.

(book 3, ch. 9)

The last words to the Dear Reader, which recall the end of *The Chimes*, though discussing the possibility of remedy, are free from optimistic flights: 'It rests with you and me, whether, in our two fields of action, similar things shall be or not.' Dickens looks forward to rebirth – in the lives of children still unborn and in deathbed repentance – but he denies Louisa a brave new life; the quiet and almost matter-of-fact language is true to the experience of the novel. His liking for cheers and congratulations at the end is subdued, as he suggests that Louisa's future will be undertaken 'as part of no fantastic vow, or bond, or brotherhood or sisterhood . . . but simply as a duty to be done.' It is particularly satisfying that Dickens avoids the pendulum-swing so grossly offensive in *Bleak House*: he does not offer the language and symbolism of strong feeling and vivid fancy in reaction to the world and values of hard fact. He matches heartless rationality with a rational warmth. The very last words of the novel are placed in a context of age and death: 'We shall sit with lighter bosoms on the hearth, to see the ashes of our fires turn grey and cold.' The image of dying fires is wholly sensitive to Coketown and remembers its ashes, in contrast to the way that Esther's little 'Bleak House' depended on ignoring the larger bleakness.

LITTLE DORRIT

Little Dorrit is a bigger and more complex venture than *Hard Times*, but the new sensibility and toughness remain and grow. Dorrit herself is no complex psychological study, but a very effective character who manages at once to be symbolic and yet also subject to time and place. She has a certain grotesqueness – stunted and sexless – that helps to stylize her as an image of virtue and to make her a more natural prison-child. She is Dickens' most successfully heroic character since Oliver Twist. And she is helped by sharing the interest of the novel with Arthur Clennam, victim of another kind of imprisonment, and a character with more inner life than we have found up to now. He too is responsively and convincingly stunted by environment, and extricates himself slowly and exhaustedly. The virtue and energy Dickens celebrates in this novel are hard-won and battered. Here too the ending is triumphant only in a muted way and has a rational sobriety and lack of crescendo. Arthur and Dorrit, like Louisa, move into a 'modest' life. The last sentence of the novel, one of the most sensitive Dickens ever wrote, musters our sympathy but makes no attempt to wipe out our recollection of all that has happened. It is

framed by the restlessness, dissatisfactions, and irre-
soluteness that have marked so much of the action: 'They
went quietly down into the roaring streets, inseparable
and blessed; and as they passed along in sunshine and
shade, the noisy and the eager, and the arrogant and the
forward and the vain, fretted, and chafed, and made their
usual uproar' (book 2, ch. 34).

The whole novel is not written or imagined with such
rational and complex control. There are flights of pity
and ecstasy where Dickens is at his worst. When the
Dorrit brothers die, for instance, Dickens has some
excellent individual touches of act and feeling, in the
account of the old man sending off his trinkets and
clothing to be pawned, and in the image of death:
'Quietly, quietly, all the lines of the plan of the great
Castle melted.' But he moves off into the banalities of
prayer – an act he simply cannot fathom – and into a
paradisal imagery that rings hollow: 'The two brothers
were before their Father; far beyond the twilight
judgments of this world; high above its mists and
obscurities.' Some of the appeals on behalf of Dorrit's
frailty and goodness also fall into banality. I emphasize
such sentimental patches because I do not want to imply
that the late Dickens is entirely in control of himself, his
characters, and his readers. There is sentimentality, but it
is not used to solve problems, reach conclusions, or
venture a grandiose finality.

Little Dorrit is like *Bleak House* in its centripetal
symbolism. The novelist draws our attention at almost
every point to the insistent symbol of imprisonment.
When we have mentioned the dark stench of the French
prison, with dazzling light outside and its microcosmic
image of class and power, the travellers in quarantine
talking explicitly of prison, the Marshalsea, Dorrit's
conceit of the grand European tour that is so like
imprisonment, the blatant but striking comparison of the
St. Bernard hostel to a prison, Mrs. Clennam's room, and
repressive religion, we have made no observations that
the novelist does not make repeatedly and clearly for us.

The scene has widened: England is like a Bleak House, human life and civilization is like a prison. The sensuous life of the symbolism is more thinly intellectual, more obviously worked out in simple equations, though it has a dimension of feeling, perhaps shown most vividly in the depression and restricted energies of Clennam, a prisoner almost incapable of stretching and moving into life. Dickens, like Henry James, makes the characters themselves do much of the symbol making, and this increases the explicitness but is at times less than plausible.

The most successful piece of institutional portraiture is not the prison, but Dickens' presentation of the civil service, then the citadel of ease and privilege, unassailed by competition, as the Circumlocution Office. Dickens creates a devastating analysis in a daring exposition – by now he could risk making speeches in the novels – and very funny satirical portraiture. The Tite Barnacle family is animated by satire that is heralded by Dickens' introductory exegis unfolding 'the Whole Science of Government.' After eleven paragraphs of sardonic commentary Dickens feels free to use ridicule:

He had a superior eye-glass dangling round his neck, but unfortunately had such flat orbits to his eyes, and such limp little eyelids, that it wouldn't stick in when he put it up, but kept tumbling out against his waistcoat buttons with a click that discomposed him very much.

(book 1, ch. 10)

The eyeglass and the limp little eyelids caricature the affectation and feebleness of this ruling class, but there is the extra comic detail so dear to Dickens in the flat orbits of the eyes. The language accurately imitates upper-class vagueness and polite exclamatoriness in its many 'I says' and 'Look heres' accompanied by the mannerism of the clicking eyeglass. Light comedy is not an end in itself; the lightness here suggest the silliness and frivolity of what is described. The levity is part of reproach and bitter criticism. It is also found in *Little Dorrit's* less grim and harsh comedy. It would be hard to imagine Flora Finching and her aunt, for instance, in *Bleak House*.

In *Little Dorrit* and *Bleak House* the comic is often neighbour to the grim or pathetic. In *Bleak House* we pass innocently from chat about tainted chops to the grisly scene of spontaneous combustion. In these novels Dickens seems to be able to infect one feeling with another, so that we scarcely know whether to call the fun grisly or the horror the more macabre for the presence of laughter. Dickens' imagination was always attracted by mixtures of feeling, and the mixtures grow richer in the late novels. The suicide of Merdle, the financier whose soiled name, taken from *merde*, gives him away, is preluded by some light comedy of manners in Fanny's drawing room. It must be remembered that Fanny is a recent graduate from prison:

> 'I thought I'd give you a call, you know.'
> 'Charmed, I am sure,' said Fanny.
> 'So I am off,' added Mr. Meddle, getting up. 'Could you lend me a penknife?'
> It was an odd thing, Fanny smilingly observed, for her who could seldom prevail upon herself even to write a letter, to lend to a man of such vast business as Mr. Merdle. 'Isn't it?' Mr. Merdle acquiesced; 'but I want one; and I know you have got several little wedding keepsakes about, with scissors and tweezers and such things in them. You shall have it back tomorrow.'
> 'Edmund,' said Mrs. Sparkler, 'open (now, very carefully, I beg and beseech, for you are so very awkward) the mother of pearl box on my little table there, and give Mr. Merdle the mother of pearl penknife.'
> 'Thank you,' said Mr. Merdle; 'but if you have got one with a darker handle, I think I should prefer one with a darker handle.'
> 'Tortoise-shell?'
> 'Thank you,' said Mr. Merdle; 'yes. I think I should prefer tortoise-shell.'
>
> (book 2, ch. 24)

Undertaking not to get ink on the knife, he goes off to kill himself. Both *Bleak House* and *Little Dorrit* are novels of multiple action, organized not only by central symbols

Mr. Merdle a borrower

Little Dorrit
Phiz

but by an operatic intricacy of plot, which is slowly and mysteriously wound and rapidly unwound. As early as *Oliver Twist* and *Barnaby Rudge* Dickens had used complicated intrigue, mystery, and unravelling, but in *Bleak House* and *Little Dorrit* such plots cover a huge range of characters, and the mystery and final revelation involve almost everyone of importance. Separate threads of action, character, and society are gathered up in plot as well as symbolism and theme. The last curtain can then be economically inclusive. The argument takes in the love story, the criminal adventure, and the satire on institutions. Dickens often creates a symbol that figures his structure as well as contributing to it. For example, the imagery of roads begins in the first chapter of *Little Dorrit*, and the prison-keeper sings, 'Who passes by this road so late? Compagnon de la Majolaine,' in a suitable overture for a novel concerned with many journeys. In the late novels journeys are not what they were in early Dickens, now forming only a part, not mapping the total trajectory. The shadows of the future, the approaching strangers, and the hysterically mounting echoes cast typically dark and ominous gloom in the dark novels. The episodic structure of journey-novels gives way to the symbol of the journey.

A TALE OF TWO CITIES

A Tale of Two Cities contains not only this imagery of an ominous future, in which the sound of revolution is gathering, but something of the prison mood and claustrophobia of *Dorrit*. It is chiefly interesting for feeling and atmosphere, and stands out, like *Barnaby Rudge* among the early novels, as a tale of action and adventure. It is also, as *Barnaby Rudge* is not, a rather feeble novel. It is bound together by symbolism and plot; it has some interesting psychological ideas, but no satiric or comic power and very little character interest. Its contemporaneity is plain in the fine opening oratory and in its Carlylean inspiration and source. It is stark in moral action, simple in feeling, quite a good novel to read in childhood, but one that does not wear well into adult life. Its most characteristic defect is in language. Like George Eliot's *Romola* (1862–1865), it suffers from the double artificiality of mimicking the language of another time and another country. Dickens usually relies heavily on the colours of language, but in this novel the characters' speech is stilted and characterless. Even where it is relieved by pseudo-translation from the French, of a mildly entertaining kind, the relief soon palls. There are some good passages, like Manette's traumatic reversions to prison life or the knitting of Madame Defarge (another emblem of tragic destiny), and there is the good idea, which degenerates into mere plot manipulations, of the physical likeness and moral unlikeness of Darnay and Carton. But the flatness and hollowness of character and reliance on external action are not typical of this period, or even of Dickens' work as a whole. It belongs with some of his feebly melodramatic stories such as *Hunted Down* (1859), which also lack density of language and character.

GREAT EXPECTATIONS

This lapse is followed by *Great Expectations*, one of Dickens' finest novels. It is remarkably dense and subtle in its dramatic psychology. It is a profound study of the theme of the bad mother and the unloved child, which Edmund Wilson has related to Dickens' own feelings of hostility and deprivation. Once more we have a solitary orphan, no longer the victim of impersonal institutions, but uncomfortably shuttling between the unloving and effective Mrs. Joe and the loving and ineffective Joe. The personal story is certainly not shut off from society, and it offers a complex analysis through character, plot, symbol, and fable. The grotesque characters of Miss Havisham and Magwitch are brought together in a conflict of class and wealth that accumulates its farce through many particulars.

The plot is one of Dickens' best, at once intricate and lucid, highly original, yet commanding the immediate assent of fable. Pip moves innocently into the convict's orbit of gratitude, need, ambition, and power, when he first innocently and spontaneously blesses the broken 'wittles' and hopes that Magwitch is enjoying the stolen food. The convict chokes at the first words of hospitality and love he has ever heard, and Pip's life begins to be ironically remade. At first, before he comes into money, he submits to a growing consciousness of class that destroys his spontaneous warmth and generosity. When he is contemptuously fed like a dog in Miss Havisham's yard, he begins his hard education in class antagonism and great expectations. This is the loss of innocence in a world where love requires the right manners, the right accent, the right clothes, and the right income. Dickens sets up this world and explores it with irony and regret. Magwitch is the fairy godfather who pays for Pip's education and thus lets him act out the fantasy of becoming a gentleman who will please Estella. It is a novel where separate fantasies struggle and defeat each other: Miss Havisham's mad dream of creating a heartless girl who will act out her need for sexual revenge locks with the convict's fantasy of making the gentleman he himself can never be. The plots of Magwitch and Miss Havisham, and their intentions and fantasies, cross. Magwitch has made a gentleman who cannot stand his table manners; Miss Havisham finds that the destruction of the heart means that Estella can make no exception for her. Pip's discovery of his real benefactor is one of the best recognition scenes in Dickens, because its shock also marks a moment of moral discovery. It leads to the conversion of Pip, to his forced intimacy with Magwitch, which, after all, becomes love.

Estella's education and perversion – a little like Louisa's – are shown from the outside, as is her eventual change of heart. Pip's is shown from the inside, in a confessional self-analysis in which he bares his secret life and its causality. It is easy to overrate this analysis, simply because it is on a larger scale and more detailed than anything else in Dickens. But it has its weakness: Pip is too clearly and completely aware of the social and emotional forces that have made him what he is. His process and motivation are available to him in a way that is not implausible, but is just not related to his individual limitations. It is a first-person novel that could really do with an omniscient author possessed of more wisdom than the hero. Pip is not endowed with anything like the sensitive register of consciousness that we find in, say, George Eliot's Maggie Tulliver or most of the central characters of Henry James. He is not shown, like them, in a fine psychic notation that imitates the workings of the brain that feels and the heart that thinks. We do not see him breaking down old categories and emerging into new ones, like Maggie or James's Strether. This is, of course, an invidious comparison, but I make it in order to stress that *Great Expectations* is a great psychological novel of Dickens' own kind. Here he explores the inner life more tenaciously than anywhere else, but it is not the kind of psychological novel that imitates the activity of the mind. It describes and symbolizes the moral life, but does not analyze its processes.

Great Expectations, like *David Copperfield*, is a novel of memory, and as such blurs character and personality in a way both convenient and evasive. Pip's story is told through the medium of recollection, and Pip is not shown as an unpleasant and obtuse snob, but always seen through the memory and sensibility of his unsnobbish older self. This technique makes his development and change of heart rather remote and shadowy, though there are impressive moments of moral feeling, as when he suddenly sees himself in relation to Joe and Magwitch, as someone who has failed in love and loyalty. As so often in Dickens, the outline of development and unpheaval is firm and plain, the detail omitted. We see the moral action in the simple action of a fable: Pip is moved by seeing his opposite in Magwitch, his double in Estella; Miss Havisham is moved by recognizing in Pip a victim of love like herself. We tend to overlook the absence of a direct dramatization of the unregenerate Pip, and he is really much the same all the way through, imaginative, sensitive, self-critical, telling us but not showing us that he was different once. The places where the unconverted Pip shows through tend, not surprisingly, to be in dialogue, like the passage where he tries to tell Biddy that it would be a good thing if Joe could attempt some self-improvement. The first-person narrative is something Dickens never used with the ease and consistency of Charlotte Brontë or Thackeray.

One of the successes of the novel, however, is its fusion of the individual story with the social indictment. Dickens shows in Pip the natural unconditioned life of the heart and the socially destructive process that weakens and distorts it, transforming instinct into calculation, human love into manipulation, generosity into greed, spontaneity into shame and ambition. Though he may be thought to soften the class issue by the pastoral image of Joe and his forge, which begs the whole question of economic determinism, he also produces some striking criticisms and ironies. Pip's ambitions as he climbs to the top are soiled by the tainted money typical of his society, but the process and some of the social and emotional changes involved will be relevant in a meritocracy. Joe and Biddy are not often patronized; they have dignity and toughness; they are not babies like Sleary, but inhabit the adult world. The end originally planned by Dickens would have kept Estella and Pip apart, though even this version reveals optimism in Pip's ability to break with his social conditioning and start again, with the far from slight advantage of a good bourgeois education. Both the old and the revised endings are modest and unassuming, like those of *Hard Times* and *Little Dorrit*: Pip and Estella are sad and scarred, and the last words of the book evoke darkness as well as light. Dickens simplifies the social issues, certainly, but the indictment of society remains.

Pip waits on Miss Haversham

Great Expectations
M. Stone

Our Mutual Friend is also a conversion story with social significance. It too deals with class, wealth, and social mobility. Plot and moral action are tightly bound in a multiple action that takes us back to *Bleak House* and *Little Dorrit*. Like *Great Expectations* it concerns a moral ordeal and test, though in this novel the test is set by the characters. The plot makers within the novel are not frustrated, or perverse, or innocent, and they come out as rather flat, like Harmon Rokesmith, or as cosy caricatures, like the Boffins. Harmon stages the pseudo-conversion of Boffin, the Golden Dustman whose heart of gold becomes – Midas-like – chilled and hardened. This impersonated corruption acts as a test and a warning to Bella Wilfer, a nice girl with mercenary leanings. The false conversion brings about the true one, and Bella rejects money and chooses love. In this novel Dickens separates the subjects of money and class, dealing with them in different actions, though there is plenty of linking material in the chorus of Veneerings and Podsnaps. The story of Bella and the Boffins might have involved class but is simply a fable about love and money, whereas the story of Lizzie Hexam and her rival lovers deals expressly with problems of changing social strata. Bradley Headstone, the repressed, respectable, and passionate schoolmaster, is opposed to Eugene Wrayburn, the idle, debilitated, able, and perverse gentleman. Backed by Charley, Lizzie's clever and ambitious brother, these characters act out a splendid crime of passion, which is thickly detailed and documented as determined by social forces.

The several mysteries, some overt, some covert, are less unified than the action of *Bleak House*: there is the impersonation of Rokesmith by Harmon, the impersonation of a miser by Boffin, which goes back to *Martin Chuzzlewit*, the story of the crime, and rich supporting material, grotesque, comic, pathetic, and satiric. The best thing in the novel is the psychological study of crime, not exactly new in Dickens – who had long ago shown Sikes's solitude and guilt as he fights the fire and listens to the cheap-jack selling stain-remover, and a little later, Jonas Chuzzlewit and his telltale heart – but new in its careful sociological backing. In the analysis of Bradley he moves out of the so-called criminal classes to draw a new kind of meritocratic monster whose violence, repression, and jealousy are part of a deadly struggle for respectability and sexuality in a not very intelligent man of strong passions with a need for social conformity. Dickens' method seems deceptively simple, using socio-psychological analysis, on the one hand, and expressive stage gestures like the beating of a hand on a stone, on the other. But what is admirable and far from simple is the blend of thriller and social criticism with the control of contrary feelings, such as we find in the scene with the tortoise-shell penknife. During the scene in Bradley's schoolroom, for instance, Rogue Riderhood enters in the grimly ridiculous guise of a friendly visitor wanting to put the children through their paces. The well-drilled chorus of children chirping their facts speaks fully for the education that has shaped Bradley, and provides just the right surface of innocent routine that Riderhood can threateningly play with and then destroy, after a tensely mounting examination not unlike his namesake Red Ridinghood's interrogation of the wolf.

But the novel as a whole lacks the force of such individual scenes. Despite the story of crime and punishment, the character of Wrayburn, and the excellent comedy of Wegg and Venus, a pair of grotesques from the mediaeval morality plays, there is much flat, undeveloped action and softness of character, with an unsatisfactory relation between the whole and its parts. Wrayburn marries Lizzie, perhaps to denote a new flexibility in attitudes to marriage between the classes, as Humphry House suggests, though with crucial stages in his conflict and decision blurred by grave illness and a symbolic rescue from death and the river. His marriage is finally approved by Twemlow, a choric character of some importance, a 'real' gentleman among the upstart rich, and an interesting new stereotype created by Dickens, the *gentleman* with a heart of gold. Although the novel is bristling with convincing social victims like Charley Hexam and Bradley, its converted or virtuous characters are much less credible. Dickens' densely documented analysis of Bradley only shows up the dreaminess of such figures as Bella and the Boffins, and even Eugene has to be helped over the tricky area of decision by symbolic action. The striking and impressive figures of the Podsnaps, the Lammles, and the Veneerings act out their own little drama and thus become much more than a comic chorus; they create a satiric action that is much closer to Thackeray's powerful caricature of a whole world, in *The Newcomes* (1854–1855), than anything else in Dickens. If *Bleak House* moves us through pity and disgust and *Little Dorrit* through ironic claustrophobia, *Our Mutual Friend* moves us through the sharpest and most strident criticism Dickens ever created. It is satire that appears on the margin of previous novels but takes over in this novel; it creates a world in which the benevolent softnesses of Mr. Wilfer the Cherub, and Bella's baby, and Wrayburn's marriage, and little Johnny's words in the Children's Hospital about 'the boofer lady,' shrivel up before our eyes. The best that we can find in this world is the likely alliance of the Lammles, taken in and making the best of things, or of Jenny Wren, with her sustaining fantasy of the father who is a bad child.

Dickens creates such a powerful anatomy of a corrupting society, ruled and moved by greed and ambition, that the wish-fulfilling fantasies of virtue and conversion are too fragile to support faith. That contemptuous insight out of which he drew Podsnap's humours and the rich (but not excremental) dust heaps where the scavenging Wegg prods with his wooden leg is realized in sensuous detail and appropriate language. Dickens can make virtue lisp like a baby or rhapsodize like a saint, but it seldom speaks with the unerring individual tones of Podsnap's loud, patronizing complacency, or the drunken ellipses of Doll's, or the soaring 'tones of moral grandeur' of the Lammles' duet. Virtue often speaks in the neutral language that expresses neither personality nor class, as in Mrs. Boffin or Lizzie, where style glosses over the social difficulties of class and marriage. Boffin the miser is so much more sharply incised in manners and speech – 'Scrunch or be scrunched' – than Boffin the good old man that it is not surprising that George Gissing (mistakenly) thought Dickens must have really intended to make the Golden Dustman a study in deterioration. Betty Higden is endowed with a certain life because she is given a language, and she is perhaps the most effective instance of virtuous energy in the book. The others are either nonentities or unappealing: Bella does not want to be the doll in the doll's house, but her marriage and maternity are nothing if not embarrassingly doll-like. Neither the action nor the psychology of individual goodness is strong enough to heal those sore spots shown and painfully touched in pity and violence and satire.

EDWIN DROOD

Dickens died after six monthly parts of *Edwin Drood* had come out. This last novel begins as a more concentrated and specialized mystery story than anything else he wrote, and it is likely that the central interest would have developed from the contrast between John Jasper's respectable public life and his secret drug-taking criminality, perhaps related to the practices of the Thugs, in which there was some contemporary interest. Edmund Wilson gives a good account of those many scholarly speculations that naturally sprang up to complete a detective story left unfinished. It is tempting but dangerous to suggest, as some have done, that Jasper is to be a study in dual personality, and I can see little in the suggestion that the detective, Datchery, is Helena Landless in disguise, but the novel's chief pleasure must lie in such speculations. It also has the interest of muted language and character. It is probably the one Dickens novel from which one could quote passages not immediately recognizable as Dickensian; and two of its characters, Mr. Grewgious and Mr. Crisparkle, are interestingly sober treatments of eccentrics who would in an earlier novel have been more exaggeratedly comic: Dickens develops them steadily and respectfully, in an almost Trollopian combination of the serious and slightly comic portrait. But it is only a marvellous fragment, the unfinished novel of an author who wrote hand to mouth, even if with a sense of design.

CONCLUSION

Robert Garis, in *The Dickens Theatre*, has discussed that frank and open theatricality with which Dickens presents and animates his work. Theatricality is a useful word to describe the vitality and flourish of his appearances as an author, and useful too in defining the limits of his art. We should insist on these limits not because Dickens has been over-praised, but in order to try to recognize his individuality. He is theatrical, for instance, in his use of external action. His stage is not often the lonely stage of soliloquy, but a stage crowded with the lively, stereotyped, stagey, concrete, simplified, physically exciting actions of actors. Dickens provides not only script and stage directions but movement and performances too. His novels are like plays in action. But in the novels from *Dombey and Son* onward, he seems to be pushing this theatrical and extrovert art beyond the limits of theatricality. The attempt to imply the inner life of characters can be traced back to Sikes and Ralph Nickleby, but becomes fully developed in Dombey and Edith, who are shown stagily but subtly. It continues in the figure of Esther Summerson whom Dickens is trying to create from the inside, though often with the unhappy result of making a reserved and introspective character behave like a self-conscious puppet. *Bleak House* is a valiant failure in an attempt to show the inner life of a human being in one part of the novel, and an impersonal, fierce vision of social injustice in the other. In *Hard Times* he places his analysis of the inner life most courageously and effectively in a simple fable and shows it, as in *Dombey and Son*, not through the technique of enlarged soliloquy, where he is generally weak, but through implication and reticence, where he is strong.

The psychology becomes more complex and mobile in content as he goes on experimenting in form: in *Little Dorrit* we have the inner self of Clennam's vivid ordinariness, and Dickens moves from this success to others, in Pip and Wrayburn. He is exploring a kind of character really belonging to another kind of novel, very far from theatrical, that novel of inner action written by Charlotte Brontë, George Eliot, George Meredith, and Henry James, where the very form of the novel takes on the imprint of consciousness. Dickens' persistent experiments are marked by a limitation. He is apparently not trying to write whole novels of inner action, but inserting this inner analysis of complexity into *his* kind of novel, placing its subtlety under the spotlight that glares on the Dickens stage. Sometimes he can only bring it off for short stretches, as with the childhood of David; sometimes he manages the marvellous sleight-of-hand that makes us feel we have had full access to the conflicts of Dombey, Edith and Louisa. Sometimes he creates the dense particularity of Pip, Clennam, Wrayburn. But it is a dense particularity revealed by his own weird spotlight. And it keeps strange company, which is not complex or dense, or always very individualized. It is the story of an an inner life, rather than the presentation of an inner life.

It points to three things: first, to that theatrical and extrovert nature of his genius. Next, it reveals his delight in difficulty, in the strenuousness spoken of by Henry James that shows itself so energetically in Dickens' attempt to push beyond the frontiers of his genius. Finally, it is no accident that in those novels where he succeeds in actualizing a central character, we feel least troubled by the duality and disparity of his analysis of the individual and the society. His developing interest in psychology seems at times to go against the grain of his genius, but in fact his sociological imagination needed the particulars of a sense of character and is badly betrayed and isolated when Dickens fails to anatomize the single heart. It is that powerful sociological imagination that triumphs most truthfully when Dickens succeeds in piercing through to the inner life. Dickens the man was often muddled, inconsistent, and neurotic in his responses to political problems and social experience, but at its best his art overcame or sublimated the weaknesses of the artist.

The Publishers wish to acknowledge with thanks the following for their help in providing the illustrations . . . Mrs. G. Abernethy, Dickens House, John Freeman & Co. and the Tate Gallery.

CHARLES DICKENS

A Select Bibliography by Graham Handley

Place of publication London unless otherwise stated. Detailed bibliographical information is to be found in the *New Cambridge Bibliography of English Literature* (Volume III) pp. 779-850. This entry (by Philip Collins) was separately issued by the Dickens Fellowship in 1970.

Any selection from the mass of material on Dickens must be arbitrary, but I would like to acknowledge here the bibliographies of K. J. Fielding, Trevor Blount and Michael Slater in the *Writers and Their Work* studies of Dickens, as well as the generous help of Andrew Sanders, editor of *The Dickensian*).

* Essential reading   + Strongly recommended

Bibliography

DICKENSIANA: a bibliography of the literature relating to Dickens and his writings, by F. G. Kitton (1886).

THE NOVELS OF CHARLES DICKENS: a bibliography and a sketch, by F. G. Kitton (1897).

THE MINOR WRITINGS OF CHARLES DICKENS: a bibliography and a sketch by F. G. Kitton (1900). *Hard Times* is listed in the minor writings.

FIRST AND EARLY AMERICAN EDITIONS OF THE WORKS OF DICKENS, by W. G. Wilkins, Cedar Rapids, Iowa (1910).

A BIBLIOGRAPHY OF THE WORKS OF CHARLES DICKENS: bibliographical, analytical and statistical, by T. Hatton and A. H. Cleaver (1933). Covers works by Dickens published at some time in monthly parts from *Sketches by Boz*, to *Edwin Drood*.

THE DICKENS STUDENT AND COLLECTOR: a list of writings about Charles Dickens and his works, 1836-1945, by W. Miller (1946). Supplements 1947, 1953. Contemporary reviews, dramatizations and plagiarisms of Dickens.

*THE DICKENS CRITICS, ed. G. H. Ford and Lauriat Lane Jnr, New York (1961).

—discussions and list of Dickens criticism 1840-1960.

+VICTORIAN FICTION: A GUIDE TO RESEARCH, ed. Lionel Stevenson, Cambridge, Mass. (1964). Contains 'Charles Dickens' by A. B. Nisbet, a comprehensive coverage of criticism (including foreign studies) and scholarship.

+VICTORIAN FICTION: A SECOND GUIDE TO RESEARCH, ed. George H. Ford, The Modern Language Association of America, New York (1978). As above, with Philip Collins evaluating the range of work on Dickens 1963–75.

THE STATURE OF DICKENS: a centenary bibliography, by J. Gold, Toronto, (1974).

VICTORIAN BIBLIOGRAPHY: published annually in the June number of *Victorian Studies*, Bloomington, Indiana, cumulative volumes covering current research 1932–1964.

+THE YEAR'S WORK IN DICKENS STUDIES: published annually in *The Dickensian* (1968–).

THE DICKENS CHECKLIST: published quarterly in each issue of *The Dickens Studies Newsletter*, Louisville, Kentucky (1970– . In progress.) Covers books, articles, reprints, dissertations about Dickens.

THE ENGLISH NOVEL: SELECT BIBLIOGRAPHICAL GUIDES ed. A. E. Dyson (1974). *Dickens* by Michael Slater, covers Dickens scholarship and criticism 1836–1971.

BIBLIOGRAPHY OF DICKENSIAN CRITICISM, 1836–1975, by R. C. Churchill.

Collected Editions

WORKS, 17 vols. (1847–68)

—first 'cheap' edition, some new prefaces by the author.

LIBRARY EDITION, 22 vols. (1858–9)

—re-issued 1861–74 in 30 vols.

THE CHARLES DICKENS EDITION, 21 vols. (1867–74) – descriptive headlines on right-hand pages.

HOUSEHOLD EDITION, 22 vols. (1871–79) – issued in monthly parts.

MACMILLAN EDITION, 21 vols. (1892–1925) – introductions by Charles Dickens Jnr.

—includes *Letters*, ed. G. Hogarth and M. Dickens.

GADSHILL EDITION, 36 vols. (1897–1908) – introduction, notes by Andrew Lang.

—contains many of Dickens uncollected articles.

NATIONAL EDITION, 40 vols. (1906–08) – ed. B. W. Matz.

NONESUCH EDITION, 23 vols. (1937–8) – includes 3 vols. of *Letters* (ed. W. Dexter) and 2 vols. of 'Collected Papers'.

+THE NEW OXFORD ILLUSTRATED DICKENS, 21 vols. (1947–58).

*CLARENDON EDITION, 5 vols. (1966– . In progress) – the definitive text of each novel based on the study of surviving manuscripts and proofs, and collation of lifetime editions. Includes textual variants, Dickens' number-plans, relevant bibliographical material. General editors, Kathleen Tillotson and James Kinsley. Published so far: *Oliver Twist* (1966), *The Mystery of Edwin Drood* (1972), *Dombey and Son* (1974), *Little Dorrit* (1979), *David Copperfield* (1981).

Biography, Letters, Speeches, Readings
(i)*THE LIFE OF CHARLES DICKENS, by John Forster, 3 vols. (1872-4), revised edition, 2 vols. (1876). 2 vols., ed. A. J. Hoppé (1969), with additional material.

CHARLES DICKENS AS I KNEW HIM, by George Dolby (1885) – Dickens' reading tours.

CHARLES DICKENS, BY HIS ELDEST DAUGHTER, By M. Dickens (1885) – later issued as MY FATHER AS I RECALL HIM (1897).

THE DICKENS CIRCLE, by J. W. T. Ley (1918).

MEMORIES OF MY FATHER, by Sir H. F. Dickens (1928).

DICKENS AND DAUGHTER, by G. Storey (1939).

CHARLES DICKENS 1812–1870, by Una Pope-Hennessy (1945).

+CHARLES DICKENS, HIS TRAGEDY AND TRIUMPH, by Edgar Johnson, New York (1952), reprinted 1965. Revised 1 vol. edition, Penguin Books, 1977.

DICKENS AND ELLEN TERNAN, by Ada Nisbet, California (1952), Cambridge (1953).

GEORGINA HOGARTH AND THE DICKENS CIRCLE, by A. A. Adrian (1957).

CHARLES DICKENS: A PICTORIAL BIOGRAPHY, by J. B. Priestley (1961).

CHARLES DICKENS: AN AUTHENTIC ACCOUNT OF HIS LIFE AND TIMES, by M. Fido (1970).

*THE WORLD OF CHARLES DICKENS, by Angus Wilson (1970).

DICKENS: A LIFE, by Norman and Jeanne MacKenzie (1979).

DICKENS AND WOMEN, by Michael Slater (1983).

(ii) THE LETTERS OF CHARLES DICKENS, ed. Walter Dexter, 3 vols. (1938).

—part of the Nonesuch edition – see above under *Collected Editions.*

LETTERS FROM CHARLES DICKENS TO ANGELA BURDETT COUTTS, 184-62, ed. Edgar Johnson (1953). First published in New York as THE HEART OF CHARLES DICKENS (1952).

*THE LETTERS OF CHARLES DICKENS (THE PILGRIM EDITION) Oxford (1965-   . In progress). Editors Madeline House, Graham Storey, Kathleen Tillotson and others. Published so far: Vol. 1, 1820–39 (1965); vol. 2, 1840–41 (1969); vol. 3, 1842–3 (1974); vol. 4, 1844–6 (1977); vol. 5, 1847–9 (1981). The edition will run to more than a dozen vols. providing the definitive texts of over 13,000 letters.

*THE SPEECHES OF CHARLES DICKENS, ed. K. J. Fielding (1960) – definitive text – later supplementary material by Philip Collins and David A. Roos in *The Dickensian* (May 1977).

*CHARLES DICKENS: THE PUBLIC READINGS, ed. Philip Collins (1975) – first complete edition of the texts of the public readings.

Periodicals devoted to Dickens

+THE DICKENSIAN, ed. Andrew Sanders (1905-   . In progress) Published three times a year since 1957. Articles (sometimes illustrated) on Dickens's life and works, book reviews, notes, reports on Dickens Fellowship activities and events. Analytical index to the first 70 vols. of the magazine by F. T. Dunn (1976).

DICKENS STUDIES, ed. N. C. Peyrouton, Boston, Mass. (1965–69).   —initially three times a year (1965–6), then biannually).

DICKENS STUDIES ANNUAL, ed. R. B. Partlow Jnr, Illinois (1970-   . In progress).

+THE DICKENS STUDIES NEWSLETTER, ed. Duane DeVries, William Axton and J. Meckier, Kentucky (1970-   . In progress).

Separate Works, publication, editions, selected criticism

(See particularly +*Dickens: The Critical Heritage*, ed. Philip Collins (1971) and +T. W. Hill's series of explanatory notes on some of the novels which appeared in *The Dickensian* in the following years: *Dombey and Son* (1942); *David Copperfield* (1943); *Bleak House* (1943–4); *Hard Times* (1952); *Little Dorrit* (1945–6); *A Tale of Two Cities* (1945); *Great Expectations* (1957–60); *Our Mutual Friend* (1947); *The Mystery of Edwin Drood* (1944)).

SKETCHES BY BOZ: 2 vols. (1836) *Essays* – second series, 1 vol. (1836), both series, 1 vol. (1839).

—DICKENS' APPRENTICE YEARS by D. De Vries, New York (1976).

—CHARLES DICKENS AND GEORGE CRUIKSHANK (Hillis Miller) (1971).

—THE OTHER NATION: THE POOR IN ENGLISH NOVELS OF THE 1840's AND 1850's by G. Smith, (1980).

THE POSTHUMOUS PAPERS OF THE PICKWICK CLUB, edited by 'Boz' (1837).

Novel. (Most of Dickens' novels were issued in monthly numbers, the last two parts – XIX and XX – being a double number of 48 pages (single numbers had 32). PICKWICK PAPERS ran from April 1836 to November 1837).

+—THE MORAL ART OF DICKENS by B. Hardy (1970).

—Penguin English Library edition (1972) ed. Patten, introduction and notes.

—*The Dickensian* (1973), article by Rachel Trickett.

OLIVER TWIST; or, the parish boy's progress, 3 vols. (1838), published as a serial in *Bentley's Miscellany* from February 1837 to April 1839 (no publication during June 1837, October 1837 and September 1838).

*—Clarendon edition ed. Kathleen Tillotson (1966).

+—Penguin English Library edition ed. Peter Fairclough (introduction by Angus Wilson) (1966).

—*The Dickensian* (1974), *Oliver Twist* issue.

*—THE PUBLIC READINGS, ed. P. Collins (1975) – includes description of Dickens' own fascination for the 'Sikes and Nancy' text and his performance.

THE LIFE AND ADVENTURES OF NICHOLAS NICKLEBY (1839) *Novel.*

—issued in twenty (as nineteen) monthly parts from April 1838 to October 1839.

*—Penguin English Library Edition (M. Slater) 1978.

+—Michael Slater's number-length monograph which accompanies the Scolar Press facsimile of the part issue (1973), 'The Composition and Monthly Publication of *Nicholas Nickleby*'.

—DICKENS FROM PICKWICK TO DOMBEY by S. Marcus (1965).

+—THE MELANCHOLY MAN by J. Lucas (1970).

MASTER HUMPHREY'S CLOCK, 3 vols. (1840–1). *Novels, sketches, short stories.*

—issued in eighty-eight weekly parts, and in monthly parts, from 4th April 1840.

THE OLD CURIOSITY SHOP (1841) *Novel.*

—in the *Clock* from 25 April 1840.

+—Penguin English Library Edition (ed. Angus Easson, introduction by Malcolm Andrews, 1972).

—*Dickens Studies Annual* (1970), 'From Manuscript to Print', by Angus Easson.

BARNABY RUDGE: a tale of the riots of 'eighty' (1841). *Novel.*

—in the *Clock* from 13th February 1841.

+—Penguin English Library edition ed. Gordon Spence (1973).

—THE DICKENS MYTH by G. Thurley (1976).

—DICKENS FROM PICKWICK TO DOMBEY by S. Marcus (1965).

—THE INIMITABLE DICKENS by A. E. Dyson (1970).

AMERICAN NOTES, for general circulation, 2 vols. (1842). *Travel.*

THE LIFE AND ADVENTURES OF MARTIN CHUZZLEWIT (1844). *Novel.*

—first issued in twenty (as nineteen) monthly parts, January 1843–July 1844.

+—Penguin English Library edition ed. P. N. Furbank (1968).

+—THE MORAL ART OF DICKENS by B. Hardy (1970).

—DICKENS FROM PICKWICK TO DOMBEY by S. Marcus (1965).

—POPE, DICKENS AND OTHERS by J. Butt (1969).

—'Change in *Martin Chuzzlewit*' by Carl Woodring, in *Nineteenth Century Literary Perspectives* (ed. Clyde Ryals, 1974).

A CHRISTMAS CAROL: in prose (1843) *Short Story* – the first of the Christmas Books.

THE CHIMES: a goblin story (1844) *Short Story.*

THE CRICKET ON THE HEARTH: a fairy tale of home (1845) *Short Story.*

THE BATTLE OF LIFE (1846) *Short Story.*

—POPE, DICKENS AND OTHERS by J. Butt (1969).

+—Introductions (by Michael Slater) to the Penguin English Library *Christmas Books* (1971).

—DICKENS: SELECTED SHORT FICTION ed. Deborah Thomas (Penguin English Library 1976).

+—DICKENS: THE CRITICAL HERITAGE ed. P. Collins (1971).

PICTURES FROM ITALY (1846) *Travel.*

—first published in the *Daily News* 21st January–2nd March, with some differences, as seven 'Travelling Letters'.

DEALINGS WITH THE FIRM OF DOMBEY AND SON, WHOLESALE, RETAIL, AND FOR EXPORTATION (1848). *Novel.*

—First issued in twenty (as nineteen) monthly parts from October 1846–April 1848.

*—Clarendon edition ed. Alan Horsman (1974).

+—Penguin English Library edition ed. P. Fairclough, introduction by Raymond Williams (1970).

+—NOVELS OF THE EIGHTEEN-FORTIES by K. Tillotson (1954), (reprinted 1961).

—DICKENS FROM PICKWICK TO DOMBEY by S. Marcus (1965).

—'Dickens and *Dombey and Son*', by John Lucas in TRADITION AND TOLERANCE IN NINETEENTH CENTURY FICTION ed. J. Goode, D. Howard and J. Lucas (1966).

—DICKENS CENTENNIAL ESSAYS ed. A. Nisbet (1971).

—'An essay on *Dombey and Son*', by Lawrence Lerner in THE VICTORIANS ed. Lerner (1978).

—'Speech and non-communication in *Dombey and Son*', by Patricia Ingham, *Review of English Studies* (May 1979).

THE HAUNTED MAN AND THE GHOST'S BARGAIN (1848) *Short Story*.

+—Penguin English Library edition ed. Michael Slater (1971) (*Christmas Books* vol. 2).

THE PERSONAL HISTORY, ADVENTURES, EXPERIENCES, AND OBSERVATIONS OF DAVID COPPERFIELD . . . (1850) *Novel*.

—issued in twenty (as nineteen) monthly parts May 1849–November 1850.

*—Clarendon edition ed. Nina Burgis (1981).

—Riverside edition ed. G. H. Ford, Boston (1958).

+—Penguin English Library edition ed. Trevor Blount (1966).

+—Dickens volume, Penguin Critical Anthologies ed. Stephen Wall (1970), which reprints Virginia Woolf's essay on *David Copperfield*.

+—DICKENS THE NOVELIST by S. Monod (1967).

—DICKENS THE NOVELIST by F. R. Leavis (1970).

*—THE WORLD OF CHARLES DICKENS by Angus Wilson (1970).

—CHARLES DICKENS: DAVID COPPERFIELD, by P. Collins (1977).

A CHILD'S HISTORY OF ENGLAND, 3 vols. (1852–4) *History*.

—first appeared in *Household Words* 25 January 1851–10 December 1853.

BLEAK HOUSE (1853) *Novel*.

—first issued in twenty (as nineteen) monthly parts, March 1852–September 1853.

+—Norton Critical edition ed. G. H. Ford and S. Monod, New York (1977).

—Penguin English Library edition ed. N. Page, introduction
J. Hillis Miller (1971).
—'Dickens: the Undivided Imagination', by Morton D.
Zabel (reprinted in THE DICKENS CRITICS ed. G. Ford and L.
Lane 1961).
—'Dickens at work on *Bleak House*', by Harvey Peter
Sucksmith, *Renaissance and Modern Studies*, 9, (1965).
+—'*Bleak House*; from Faraday to Judgement Day', by A. Y.
Wilkinson, *Journal of English Literary History*, 34, June
1967.
—TWENTIETH CENTURY INTERPRETATIONS OF BLEAK HOUSE ed.
J. Korg, New Jersey 1968.
+—DICKENS: BLEAK HOUSE (Casebook Series) ed. A. E. Dyson
(1969).
—CHARLES DICKENS: BLEAK HOUSE, by G. Smith (1974).
—'The ghostly signs of *Bleak House*', by Michael Ragussis,
Nineteenth Century Fiction, 34 (December 1979).
(NOTE: *Bleak House* is Dickens' most written about novel,
and many of the general studies referred to earlier in this
bibliography have chapters or sections devoted to it).
HARD TIMES: FOR THESE TIMES (1854) *Novel.*
—first appeared in *Household Words* in weekly instalments
1st April–12th August 1854.
+—Norton Critical edition ed. G. Ford and S. Monod, New
York (1966).
+—Penguin English Library edition, ed. David Craig (1969).
—'Introduction' by George Bernard Shaw (1912), reprinted
in THE DICKENS CRITICS ed. G. Ford and L. Lane (1961).
—TWENTIETH CENTURY INTERPRETATIONS OF HARD TIMES ed.
P. E. Gray, Englewood Cliffs, N.J. (1969).
—*Hard Times*: critical commentary and notes, by Angus
Easson (1973).
LITTLE DORRIT (1857) *Novel.*
—first issued in twenty (as nineteen) monthly parts
December 1855–June 1857.
*—Clarendon edition ed. Harvey Peter Sucksmith (1976).
+—Penguin English Library edition ed. John Holloway
(1967).
—College Classics in English edition ed. R. D. McMaster
(Toronto, 1969).

—'*Little Dorrit*', by Lionel Trilling, *Kenyon Review* (Autumn 1953, reprinted as introduction to The New Oxford Illustrated Dickens *Little Dorrit* and in THE DICKENS CRITICS ed. G. Ford and L. Lane.

—'Dickens' monthly number plans for *Little Dorrit*', by P. D. Herring, *Modern Philology*, 64 (August 1966).

—CHARLES DICKENS: LITTLE DORRIT, by J. C. Reid (1967).

+—DICKENS 1970 ed. Michael Slater (article by C. P. Snow on 'Dickens and the Public Service').

—'The Radicalism of *Little Dorrit*', by William Myers in LITERATURE AND POLITICS IN THE NINETEENTH CENTURY ed. John Lucas (1971).

—REALITY AND COMIC CONFIDENCE IN CHARLES DICKENS (Scott) 1979.

REPRINTED PIECES (1858) *Essays*—vol. 8 of the Library Edition; consists of 31 articles contributed to *Household Words*.

A TALE OF TWO CITIES (1859) *Novel.*

—first published in *All The Year Round* in weekly instalments from 30 April–26 November 1859.

+Penguin English Library edition ed. George Woodcock (1970).

—CRAFT AND CHARACTER IN MODERN FICTION by M. D. Zabel, New York, (1957).

—TWENTIETH CENTURY INTERPRETATIONS OF A TALE OF TWO CITIES ed. C. E. Beckwith (New York, 1972).

+—DICKENS THE NOVELIST by S. Monod (1967).

+—THE VICTORIAN HISTORICAL NOVEL (1840–1880), by Andrew Sanders (1979).

GREAT EXPECTATIONS, 3 vols. (1861) Novel.

—first published in *All The Year Round* in weekly instalments from 1st December 1860–3rd August 1861.

+—Penguin English Library edition ed. Angus Calder (1965).

—'Introduction' and 'Postscript' to *Great Expectations*, by George Bernard Shaw. Restores Dickens' alternative ending to the novel.

—THE ENGLISH NOVEL: FORM AND FUNCTION, by Dorothy Van Ghent (New York 1953).

'On Great Expectations', an essay reprinted in DICKENS: MODERN JUDGEMENTS ed. A. E. Dyson (1968).

—ASSESSING GREAT EXPECTATIONS: MATERIALS FOR ANALYSIS, ed. R. Lettis and W. E. Morris, San Francisco (1963).

—'The Genesis of a Novel: *Great Expectations*', by Harry Stone in CHARLES DICKENS 1812–1870, ed. W. F. Tomlin.

+—THE MORAL ART OF DICKENS by B. Hardy (1970).

+—A Study Guide to *Great Expectations* AND *Great Expectations* (Units 6 and 7 of the Open University Course, *The Nineteenth Century Novel and Its Legacy*, by Graham Martin (1973).

—'Beating and Cringing: *Great Expectations*', by A. L. French, *Essays in Criticism*, 24, (April 1974).

THE UNCOMMERCIAL TRAVELLER (1861) *Essays.*

—a series of essays from *All The Year Round*, included in the Gadshill Editions (1908).

OUR MUTUAL FRIEND (1865) *Novel.*

—first issued in twenty (as nineteen) monthly parts from May 1864–November 1865.

+—Penguin English Library edition ed. Stephen Gill (1971).

—'*Our Mutual Friend*', by R. Morse, *Partisan Review*, 16, March 1949 (reprinted in THE DICKENS CRITICS (1961) and in DICKENS: MODERN JUDGEMENTS (1968).

—THE FORM OF VICTORIAN FICTION (Hillis Miller) (reprinted 1979).

+—LAUGHTER AND DESPAIR: READINGS IN TEN NOVELS OF THE VICTORIAN ERA. by U. C. Knoepflmacher (Berkeley and Los Angeles, 1971), includes '*Our Mutual Friend*: Fantasy as Affirmation'.

—DICKENS AND THE TRIALS OF THE IMAGINATION by G. Stewart, (Cambridge, Mass. 1974).

—NINETEENTH CENTURY LITERARY PERSPECTIVES: ESSAYS IN HONOUR OF LIONEL STEVENSON, ed. Ryals, N. C. 1974, (essay on *Our Mutual Friend* by Richard Altick).

—'The education of the reader in *Our Mutual Friend*', by Rosemary Mundhenk, *Nineteenth Century Fiction*, 34, June 1979.

—'Come Back and Be Alive': Living and Dying in *Our Mutual Friend*, by Andrew Sanders, *The Dickensian*, Autumn 1979.

THE MYSTERY OF EDWIN DROOD (1870) *Novel.*

—unfinished at Dickens' death. First issued in monthly parts April–September 1870 (due to be completed in twelve parts).

*—Clarendon edition ed. Margaret Cardwell (1972).

+—Penguin English Library edition ed. A. J. Cox, introduction by Angus Wilson (1974).

—'Dickens's Notebook and *Edwin Drood*', by G. H. Ford, Nineteenth Century Fiction, 6, (December 1952).

Additional Notes:

(i) *Manuscripts*

Those of most the novels are in the Forster Collection at the Victoria and Albert Museum. On the Centenary of Dickens' death in 1970 the Museum organised an exhibition (*Charles Dickens 1812–1870*) with the manuscripts forming the most important part.

The manuscript of *Great Expectations* is in the *Wisbech Museum*; that of *Our Mutual Friend* in the Pierpoint Morgan Library, New York.

(ii) In addition to his journalism and magazine contributions in the early part of his career, Dickens realised his ambition to edit his own periodical with *Household Words* (March 1850–May 1859), and *All The Year Round* (April 1859 until his death in June 1870). The book which recorded author and payments for articles in *Household Words* is at Princeton. It was edited by A. Lohrli (University of Toronto Press 1973), while Harry Stone edited *The Uncollected Writings of Charles Dickens in Household Words* 1850–59, 2 vols. (1969).

General Criticism

(*Penguin Critical Anthologies* – Charles Dickens volume ed. S. Wall 1970).

CHARLES DICKENS, by George Gissing (1898).

+CHARLES DICKENS, by G. K. Chesterton (1906).

CHARLES DICKENS, by A. C. Swinburne (1913).

DICKENS AND OTHER VICTORIANS, by A. C. Quiller-Couch, Cambridge (1925).

+ASPECTS OF THE NOVEL, by E. M. Forster (1927).

EARLY VICTORIAN NOVELISTS, by Lord David Cecil (1934).

*INSIDE THE WHALE, by George Orwell (1940) – the important essay on Dickens reprinted in CRITICAL ESSAYS (1954).

*THE WOUND AND THE BOW, by Edmund Wilson, Boston, Mass. (1941) – 'Dickens: the Two Scrooges' helped to revitalise Dickens criticism.

+DICKENS ROMANCIER, by Sylvère Monod, Paris (1953) – reprinted as DICKENS THE NOVELIST, Oklahoma (1968) – first major focus on the manuscripts and proofs of the novels.

+CHARLES DICKENS: A CRITICAL INTRODUCTION, by K. J. Fielding (1958, revised 1965).

+CHARLES DICKENS: THE WORLD OF HIS NOVELS, by J. Hillis Miller, Cambridge, Mass. (1958).

+DICKENS AND THE TWENTIETH CENTURY, ed. J. Gross and G. Pearson (1962) – essays on each work by leading critics.

+THE DICKENS THEATRE: A REASSESSMENT OF THE NOVELS, by Robert Garis (1965).

THE NARRATIVE ART OF CHARLES DICKENS: THE RHETORIC OF SYMPATHY AND IRONY IN HIS NOVELS, by Harvey Peter Sucksmith (1970).

THE MORAL ART OF DICKENS, by Barbara Hardy (1970).

DICKENS THE NOVELIST, by F. R. and Q. D. Leavis (1970).

THE INIMITABLE DICKENS: A READING OF THE NOVELS, by A. E. Dyson (1970).

+DICKENS 1970, ed. Michael Slater (1970).

+DICKENS CENTENNIAL ESSAYS, ed. Ada Nisbet and B. Nevius (1971).

DICKENS AND THE RHETORIC OF LAUGHTER, by J. Kincaid (1971) – examination of Dickens's comedy.

+THE VIOLENT EFFIGY: A STUDY OF DICKENS' IMAGINATION, by John Carey (1973).

DICKENS AND THE ART OF ANALOGY, by H. M. Daleski (1970).

+THE MELANCHOLY MAN: A STUDY OF DICKENS'S NOVELS, by John Lucas (1970, revised 1980).

(Both general and particular are present in many of the books on Dickens, and there is an inevitable overlap. Below is a list of some of the more sharply-focussed works).

DICKENS AS A READER, by W. M. C. Kent (1872) – reprinted with introduction by Philip Collins (1971).

DICKENS AND HIS ILLUSTRATORS, by F. G. Kitton (1899, reprinted Amsterdam 1972).

+THE DICKENS WORLD, by Humphrey House (1941).

*DICKENS AT WORK, by John Butt and Kathleen Tillotson (1957) – close examination of Dickens's art based on study of selected manuscripts, corrected proofs number plans.

A REVIEW OF ENGLISH LITERATURE: DICKENS NUMBER, ed. John Butt (July 1961).

+DICKENS AND CRIME, by Philip Collins (1962, new edition 1964).

*DICKENS AND EDUCATION, by Philip Collins (1963).

LOVE AND PROPERTY IN THE NOVELS OF DICKENS, by R. H. Dabney (1967).

THE LANGUAGE OF DICKENS, by G. L. Brook (1970).

+DICKENS AND FAME 1870-1970, ed. Michael Slater (1970).

THE CITY OF DICKENS, by Alexander Welsh (1971).

CHARLES DICKENS: RADICAL MORALIST, by Joseph Gold (1972).

DICKENS AND CARLYLE, by W. Oddie (1972).

IMAGERY AND THEME IN THE NOVELS OF CHARLES DICKENS, by Robert Barnard (1974).

+A KIND OF POWER: THE SHAKESPEARE-DICKENS ANALOGY, by A. Harbage (1975).

DICKENS AND MESMERISM: THE HIDDEN SPRINGS OF ACTION, by F. Kaplan (1975).

DICKENS AND THE TRIALS OF THE IMAGINATION, by Garrett Steward (1975).

DICKENS'S APPRENTICE YEARS, by Duane DeVries, New York and Harvester Press (1976).

+CHARLES DICKENS AND HIS PUBLISHERS, by Robert L. Patten (1978).

+DICKENS ON AMERICA AND THE AMERICANS, ed. Michael Slater (1978).

DICKENS AND CHARITY, by Norris Pope (1978).

DICKENS AND THE CITY, by F. S. Schwarzbach (1979).

DICKENS AND THE INVISIBLE WORLD, by Harry Stone (1979).

DICKENS AND RELIGION, by Dennis Walder (1981).

+DICKENS AND HIS ORIGINAL ILLUSTRATORS, by Jane R. Cohen (1980).

+DICKENS: INTERVIEWS AND RECOLLECTIONS ed. Philip Collins, 2 vols. (1981).

DICKENS AND WOMEN, by Michael Slater (1983).

14294